CANADIAN HUMAN RIGHTS LAW AND COMMENTARY

S. M. CORBETT, PH.D., LL.B.

Canadian Human Rights Law and Commentary
© LexisNexis Canada Inc. 2007
March 2007

This publication is designed to provide accurate and authoritative information. It is sold with the understanding that the publisher is not engaged in rendering legal, accounting or other professional advice. If legal or other expert advice is required, the services of a competent professional should be sought. The analysis contained herein represents the opinions of the author(s) and should in no way be construed as being either official or unofficial policy of any government body.

Members of the LexisNexis Group worldwide

Canada	LexisNexis Canada Inc, 123 Commerce Valley Dr. E., MARKHAM, Ontario
Argentina	Abeledo Perrot, Jurisprudencia Argentina and Depalma, BUENOS AIRES
Australia	Butterworths, a Division of Reed International Books Australia Pty Ltd, CHATSWOOD, New South Wales
Austria	ARD Betriebsdienst and Verlag Orac, VIENNA
Chile	Publitecsa and Conosur Ltda, SANTIAGO DE CHILE
Czech Republic	Orac sro, PRAGUE
France	Éditions du Juris-Classeur SA, PARIS
Hong Kong	Butterworths Asia (Hong Kong), HONG KONG
Hungary	Hvg Orac, BUDAPEST
India	Butterworths India, NEW DELHI
Ireland	Butterworths (Ireland) Ltd, DUBLIN
Italy	Giuffré, MILAN
Malaysia	Malayan Law Journal Sdn Bhd, KUALA LUMPUR
New Zealand	Butterworths of New Zealand, WELLINGTON
Poland	Wydawnictwa Prawnicze PWN, WARSAW
Singapore	Butterworths Asia, SINGAPORE
South Africa	Butterworth Publishers (Pty) Ltd, DURBAN
Switzerland	Stämpfli Verlag AG, BERNE
United Kingdom	Butterworths Tolley, a Division of Reed Elsevier (UK), LONDON, WC2A
USA	LexisNexis, DAYTON, Ohio

Library and Archives Canada Cataloguing in Publication

Corbett, S. M. (Stanley M.), 1945-
  Canadian human rights law and commentary / Stanley Corbett.

Includes bibliographical references and index.
ISBN 978-0-433-45039-9

  1. Human rights—Canada. I. Title.

KE4381.C67 2007   342.7108'5   C2007-900006-1
KF4483.C5C67 2007

Printed and bound in Canada.

Over the long term the greatest thanks go to my family, Jane, Sean and Alison. Their affection and support have without fail exceeded beyond measure anything to which any human being might claim a right.

ABOUT THE AUTHOR

Stanley Corbett is appointed to the Faculty of Law at Queen's University. He is also a member of the Affiliated Faculty with the Queen's Centre for Health Services and Policy Research, and is an Associate Faculty member of the School of Policy Studies. He received his LL.B. in 1995. His current areas of teaching include Public and Constitutional Law, Administrative Law, Human Rights and Public International Law. In addition to his work in the Faculty of Law, he teaches Health Law in the Faculty of Health Sciences. He has also taught courses on public sector ethics in the School of Policy Studies. In 1999 he provided two background papers for the review of the *Canadian Human Rights Act*, one on the language of human rights and a second on the independence of human rights commissions. He has served as an advisor to Health Canada and, for the past several years, to the Ontario Ministry of Health and Long Term Care. More recently, he provided a research study for the Gomery Commission on the constitutional foundation of the obligation to account for government expenditures.

TABLE OF CONTENTS

TABLE OF CASES

A

B

C

D

F

L

M

N

O

P

R

S

"...may human rights become the common language of humanity."

Address by the Secretary General of the United Nations at the opening
of the World Conference on Human Rights, Vienna, 1993

COMMENTARY

I.   INTRODUCTION

> Humanity has rights superior to those of Industry and Nationality. For their ultimate solution, industrial and international problems alike await the inspiration of a universally accepted faith in human brotherhood.[1]

These words from William Lyon Mackenzie King's introduction to the revised edition of his book, *Industry and Humanity*, are dated August 7, 1947, two years and one day after the first atomic weapon fell on a civilian population at Hiroshima. This was also the date of the 1919 Liberal leadership convention at which Mackenzie King became leader of the party, and of the second convention in 1948 that would elect his replacement. As the opening words of the introduction make clear, then Prime Minister King was well aware of the pall cast by Hiroshima over that date:

> The release of atomic energy marks the opening of a new age both for Industry and for Humanity. Whether this new era will be one of unprecedented progress or of unparalleled destruction, is the question uppermost in the minds of men today.[2]

Whatever one thinks of the theory of industrial relations expounded in *Industry and Humanity*, there can be no doubt that King's concerns in this introduction were to become central themes of the second half of the last century.

King was 26, and Canada's first Deputy Minister of Labour, when the 20th century opened. He died at its mid-point, having lived through both World Wars and the Great Depression. A complex and decidedly controversial figure, he is remembered as often today for his eccentricities, as he is for his achievements during his 40 year career in politics, 21 of which he spent as Prime Minister. Yet, Adam Chapnick, the author of a recent book on the founding of the United Nations, argues that Mackenzie King played an important role in the creation of an institution that many believed represented the best hope for the future of humanity at the end of the Second World War. After persuasively demonstrating that Canada's role in the

---

[1]   W.L. Mackenzie King, *Industry and Humanity: a Study in the Principles Underlying Industrial Reconstruction*, (Toronto: The MacMillan Company, 1947) at xxix.

[2]   *Ibid.*, at xiii.

founding of the United Nations was widely exaggerated at the time, Chapnick concludes his study with the following comment:

> When Canadians look back on the origins of the United Nations, they should feel tremendous pride. ... To be Canadian in 1945 meant to be engaged in world affairs and actively concerned about the socio-economic state of less fortunate communities ... the Canada that helped to create the United Nations ... belonged to Mackenzie King.[3]

For Chapnick this conclusion is justified by the fact that Canada's most significant contribution to the *Charter of the United Nations* was "in defining and increasing the responsibilities of the institution closer to its Prime Minister's heart: the Economic and Social Council". For King, "Canada's real capacity for influence lay in the economic and social arenas".[4] Yet, three years later during the debate in the General Assembly of the United Nations over the draft version of the *Universal Declaration of Human Rights* ("U.D.H.R."),[5] the Canadian delegation "abstained in the vote on all of the economic and social rights" that were included in the U.D.H.R.[6]

When the *Charter of the United Nations* was signed on June 26, 1945 almost 22,000 Canadians of Japanese descent were living in internment camps to which they had been consigned on the basis of racist policies endorsed by Mackenzie King.[7] The *Chinese Immigration Act*[8] which effectively banned the immigration of persons from China would not be

---

[3]   Adam Chapnick, *The Middle Power Project* (Vancouver: UBC Press, 2005) at 152.

[4]   *Ibid.*, at 150.

[5]   GA Res. 217A (III), U.N. GAOR 3d Sess., Supp. No. 13, U.N. Doc A/810 (1948) 71.

[6]   William Schabas, "Canada and the Adoption of the *Universal Declaration of Human Rights*" (1998) 43 McGill L.J. 403 at para. 30. Schabas has explored the reasons for Canada's official response to the U.D.H.R., a response that reflected deep divisions within the government of the day regarding the entire human rights project.

[7]   The disconnection between King's concern for the socio-economic welfare of Canadians and the internment of his fellow citizens is chillingly illustrated by the following diary entry, dated August 6, 1945:
> It is fortunate that the use of the bomb should have been upon the Japanese rather than upon the white races of Europe.

Quoted in Ann Sunahara, *The Politics of Racism* (Toronto: Lorimer, 1981) at 19; cf. 45-46. This combination of attitudes toward human well-being was not, of course, unique to Mackenzie King. Franklin Delano Roosevelt who is best remembered for his "New Deal" programs dealing with the socio-economic well-being of those whose lives had been all but destroyed by the Great Depression, also signed an order authorizing the internment of over 100,000 Japanese Americans. For a recent discussion of FDR's motives see Greg Robinson, *By Order of the President: FDR and the Internment of Japanese Americans* (Cambridge, Mass.: Harvard University Press, 2001) at 73-124, esp. 119*ff.*

[8]   S.C. 1923, c. 38. The first statute regulating and restricting Chinese immigration to Canada had been enacted in 1885.

repealed for three more years.[9] It had been enacted in 1923 during Mackenzie King's first term as Prime Minister. In the early years of the Second World War the Supreme Court of Canada ruled in favour of a tavern owner who had refused to serve a group of men solely on the ground that they were black, or to use the term of the day, "coloured".[10] Both prior to and during the war Mackenzie King had been reluctant, at best, to challenge policies that kept Jewish refugees, including large numbers of children, from entering Canada.[11] During the war it had been illegal to be a Jehovah's Witness, or a member of any one of a number of organizations deemed subversive under orders issued by the Governor-General in Council and known as the Defence of Canada Regulations.[12]

A year after the end of the war the Federal Government would embark on yet another attempt to revise the *Indian Act*.[13] Aboriginal Canadians, having volunteered in large numbers for service during the war, returned to find things little changed on the home front.[14] Their children were being taken from them so they could be "assimilated" by means of the residential schools program.[15] Like the Japanese Canadians and the Chinese Canadians, many of them were still not allowed to vote.[16]

Two years before the end of the war the President of the Canadian Political Science Association, C.A. Dawson, drew attention to the relative racial homogeneity of the population of Canada.[17] He noted that with the exception of the French in Quebec, whose culture was protected, the rest of Canada was gradually fusing into a single culture, a process facilitated, in his view, by the absence of those biological barriers that separated Canadians of European origins from the "negro and oriental elements". He drew attention to the diverse ethnic origins of settlers on the Prairies and

---

[9] Anthony B. Chan, *Gold Mountain: The Chinese in the New World* (Vancouver: New Star Books, 1983) at 97, 142*ff*; Peter S. Li, *Chinese in Canada*, 2d ed. (Don Mills: Oxford University Press, 1998) at 34-35.

[10] The majority were clearly more offended by the fact that the men had raised objections than they were by the refusal of service: *Christie v. York Corp.*, [1940] S.C.R. 139, [1940] 1 D.L.R. 81 (S.C.C.).

[11] Irving Abella & Harold Troper, *None is Too Many* (Toronto: Lester and Orpen Dennys, 1982).

[12] William Kaplan, *State and Salvation* (Toronto: University of Toronto Press, 1989).

[13] *An Act to Amend and Consolidate the Laws Respecting Indians* ("*The Indian Act, 1876*") S.C. 1876, c. 18.

[14] J.R. Miller, *Skyscrapers Hide the Heavens: A History of Indian-White Relations in Canada*, rev. ed (Toronto: University of Toronto Press, 1991) at 220-23.

[15] J.R. Miller, *Shingwauk's Vision: A History of Native Residential Schools* (Toronto: University of Toronto Press, 1996).

[16] Chinese Canadians and Indian (South Asian) Canadians acquired the right to vote in federal elections in 1947; the franchise was extended to Japanese Canadians in 1948. The unqualified right to vote was not extended to status Indians in Canada until 1960.

[17] C.A. Dawson, "Canada in Perspective" (1943) 9 The Canadian Journal of Economics and Political Science 289.

noted that "each group (was) moving swiftly ... in the direction of A Canadian Way of Life".[18] Clearly the Canada that "belonged to Mackenzie King" had a relatively restricted definition of those who were welcome to participate in forging a "Canadian Way of Life". Concern for the socio-economic well-being of "the less fortunate communities" was not necessarily combined with the protection of civil liberties or opposition to discrimination.

In addition, while Dawson was quick to emphasize that Canada included both English and French, he also believed that the majority of immigrants would assimilate "toward the English-Speaking pattern of life". In recognizing the French fact in Canada no reference was made to the absence of the francophone community in the corridors of power. Four decades later, historian J.L. Granatstein would note with reference to the same period that there was not "a single French-Canadian member" in the highest levels of the federal civil service. He went on to say:

> [For] one of the *Charter* groups in a nation to be completely unrepresented at the top level of the bureaucracy was a true reflection of the concentration of power in Canada: only English Canadians had it. Not only were Quebecois not represented at the very top, but they were also denied a share of power at the lower levels. ... Thus government business in Ottawa was conducted in one language only ... Clerks and typists might have spoken French among themselves, but no matter how much they fumed, the work they prepared was solely in English.[19]

According to Granatstein, government business was also conducted by members of only one gender. The mandarins of Ottawa were "exclusively male". Indeed, in all sectors of the workforce, women who had been encouraged to work during the war were being discouraged from doing so on the ground that their real place was in the home. While this attempt to maintain the gender divide was to meet with limited success, government policy makers did little to facilitate the equal participation of women in the Canadian economy.[20]

Proponents of civil liberties and opponents of discrimination have not always been advocates for social and economic rights. Yet, the *Charter of the United Nations* that established the Economic and Social Council included among the statements of its purposes, the following:

> To achieve international cooperation in solving international problems of an economic, social, cultural, or humanitarian character, and in promoting and

---

[18]   *Ibid.*, at 294.

[19]   J.L. Granatstein, *The Ottawa Men: The Civil Service Mandarins, 1935-1957* (Toronto: Oxford University Press, 1982) at 4-5.

[20]   Alison Prentice *et al.*, *Canadian Women: A History* (Toronto: Harcourt Brace Jovanovich, 1988) at 303-17.

encouraging respect for human rights and for fundamental freedoms for all
without distinction as to race, sex, language, or religion. ...[21]

From the beginning the improvement of the economic and social condition
of all human beings was to be joined with the protection of civil liberties and
the fight against discrimination. The unity of this project was clearly evident
in the U.D.H.R., which provided the vocabulary for what became the most
important political movement of the second half of the 20th century.

Canada had already embarked upon the project envisaged in the
U.D.H.R. by the beginning of the second half of the 20th century.[22] The
project was carried out by those who had lived through the first half of the
century and did not want to see it repeated. During the two decades after the
end of the Second World War the provinces enacted anti-discrimination
legislation, the Federal Government enacted the *Canadian Bill of Rights*[23]
and created the Canada Pension Plan, and the provinces and the Federal
Government together established the basic framework for the universal
health insurance plan that was to become known as Medicare.[24] While these
initiatives were all consistent with Canada's commitments under the
U.D.H.R. only the anti-discrimination statutes made reference to that
document and even then, as a rule, only in their preambles. The Supreme
Court would eventually refer to anti-discrimination legislation as
fundamental or quasi-constitutional law and in 1985 the goal of eliminating
discrimination was entrenched in the Constitution by section 15 of the
Canadian Charter of Rights and Freedoms ("Charter").[25] Three years earlier
the Charter had also entrenched a range of political, legal and cultural rights,
although not in the name of human rights.

By the time the Charter was introduced the momentum of the post-war
project had begun to wane. Shortly after Canada signed the two international
covenants that were intended to transform the moral commitment of the

---

[21]   *Charter of the United Nations*, 26 June 1945, Can. T.S. 1945 No. 7 (entered into force 24
       October, 1945).
[22]   The *British North America Act, 1867* (now *Constitution Act, 1867*) was amended in 1940 to give
       the Federal Government jurisdiction over unemployment insurance. Like other sections of the
       Constitution dealing with social and economic rights, this section is a grant of power, not an
       entrenched obligation to act. The first Family Allowance (Baby Bonus) cheques were mailed
       out on July 1, 1945 (*Constitution Act, 1867* (U.K.), 30 & 31 Vict., c. 3, s. 91(2A), reprinted in
       R.S.C. 1985, App. II, No. 5).
[23]   S.C. 1960, c. 44.
[24]   Accounts of the history of Medicare in Canada may be found in M. Taylor, *Health Insurance
       and Canadian Public Policy: The Seven Decisions That Created the Canadian Health Insurance
       System and their Outcomes* (Montreal: McGill-Queen's University Press, 1988); C.D. Naylor,
       *Private Practice, Public Payment: Canadian Medicine and the Politics of Health Insurance
       1911-1966* (Montreal: McGill-Queen's University Press, 1986).
[25]   Part I of the *Constitution Act, 1982*, being Schedule B to the *Canada Act 1982* (U.K.) 1982,
       c. 11.

U.D.H.R. into a legally binding one, the goal of including social and economic rights in the Charter was postponed.[26] While the framework of Medicare was consolidated with the enactment of the *Canada Health Act*[27] in 1984, the courts have consistently held that the Charter does not obligate the government to provide services of any kind. When governments, federal or provincial, choose to act they must act in accordance with the Charter. However, the courts have ruled that there is nothing in the Charter that can be used to compel a government to act. As MacLachlin C.J. noted:

> This Court has repeatedly held that the legislature is under no obligation to create a particular benefit. It is free to target the social programs it wishes to fund as a matter of public policy, provided the benefit itself is not conferred in a discriminatory manner.[28]

Even the right of children to an education is not constitutionally protected in Canada.[29] At the beginning of the 21st century Canada's foreign aid spending remained well below the 0.7 per cent of gross domestic product to which the country had been committed since the 1960s.[30] Child poverty rates in Canada had begun to climb so that by 2004 they were higher than they had been in 1989, when the House of Commons voted unanimously to eliminate child poverty by the year 2000.[31] Canadians were debating the

---

[26] *International Covenant on Economic, Social and Cultural Rights* ("I.C.E.S.C.R."), 16 December 1966, 993 U.N.T.S. 3 (entered into force 3 January 1976, accession by Canada 19 May, 1976); *International Covenant on Civil and Political Rights* ("I.C.C.P.R."), 16 December 1966, 999 U.N.T.S. 171 (entered into force 23 March 1976, accession by Canada 19 May, 1976).

[27] R.S., 1985, c. C-6.

[28] *Auton (Guardian ad litem of) v. British Columbia (Attorney General)*, [2004] S.C.J. No. 71, [2004] 3 S.C.R. 657 at para. 41.

[29] While s. 93 of the *Constitution Act, 1867* protected the rights of Protestant and Roman Catholic minorities to education, this protection is contingent upon the creation of a school system by a province. As Iacobucci J. noted in *Adler v. Ontario*, [1996] S.C.J. No. 110, [1996] 3 S.C.R. 609 at paras 46-47:

> ... Roman Catholic parents could choose between two publicly funded educational systems — one Roman Catholic, the other non-denominational. Section 93 gives constitutional protection to this publicly funded choice. Therefore, the public school system is an integral part of the Confederation compromise and, consequently, receives a protection against constitutional or Charter attack.
>
> This protection exists despite *the fact that public school rights are not themselves constitutionally entrenched.* It is the province's plenary power to legislate with regard to public schools, which are open to all members of society, without distinction, that is constitutionally entrenched. [Emphasis added.]

[30] Measures of foreign aid are notoriously difficult and, as a result, inevitably controversial. In 2005, the Center for Global Development ranked Canada 10th out of 21 rich countries on its Commitment to Development Index. Canada ranked 13th in its direct foreign aid with a contribution rate of 0.24 per cent of GDP, well below its decades old commitment to a rate of 0.7 per cent of GDP.

[31] In its report on *Child Poverty in Rich Countries 2005*, UNICEF ranked Canada 19th out of 26 countries in terms of the number of children living in poverty. While the percentage of children

sustainability of universal health care and the Supreme Court was evenly split on the question of whether Canada's most important instrument for human rights protection, the Charter, could be used to undermine the Canadian health insurance model.[32] Meanwhile, tuition at many Canadian universities, especially in professional schools, had skyrocketed.[33] National security has once again become a readily available excuse for curtailing civil liberties and for discriminatory policies that target Canadian citizens on the basis of the behaviour of persons in other countries. Canadians, suspected of terrorist activities, were being denied basic rights that had been central to the common law for almost 1000 years.[34] Once again the concept of crime has been extended beyond the actions of individuals to include membership in an organisation.[35]

It is true that Canadians enjoy a relatively robust, although by no means perfect, anti-discrimination complaint system created by legislation enacted by the provincial, territorial and federal governments. The commissions and tribunals established under this legislation deal with complaints of discrimination in employment, accommodation and the provision of services. Furthermore, if a complainant is not satisfied with the results of this process it is possible to apply to the courts in search of a remedy. That said, discrimination is clearly still a serious problem in Canada. In a report, entitled *Visible Minorities and the Public Service of Canada*, submitted to the Canadian Human Rights Commission in 1997 it was noted that Canada's reputation as "a racially-tolerant country in the community of nations" is belied by the fact that within the federal public service visible minorities made up a significantly lower portion of those employed than they do within the workforce as a whole or, even more significantly, within the private sector. The authors of the report concluded that "such a low level of visible minority representation in (Canada's) public service is less than acceptable".[36]

---

living in poverty declined slightly during the 1990s, there is evidence that it has begun to climb again since 2000.

[32] *Chaoulli v. Quebec (Attorney General)*, [2005] S.C.J. No. 33, [2005] 1 S.C.R. 791.

[33] Marc Frenette, *The Impact of Tuition Fees on University Access: Evidence from a Large-scale Price Deregulation in Professional Programs* (Ottawa: Minister of Industry, 2005) at 21-27. Tuition in some professional programmes, particularly dentistry and medicine, increased by as much as a factor of five between 1972 and 2003. Fees had begun to stabilize by 2005, which saw the lowest increase since 1978.

[34] Under the authority of the *Immigration and Refugee Protection Act*, S.C. 2001, c. 27 permanent residents and foreign nationals may be incarcerated on the basis of security certificates that dramatically restrict their opportunities for various otherwise available legal remedies.

[35] *Criminal Code*, R.S., 1985, c. C-46, ss. 83.05, 83.18.

[36] *Visible Minorities and the Public Service of Canada*, online: Canadian Human Rights Commission <http://www.chrc-ccdp.ca/publications/chap3-en.asp>.

More recently the Canadian Labour Congress released a report, *Racial Status and Employment Outcomes*, that demonstrates the ongoing effects of racism in the private sector as well.[37] The report identified a particularly disturbing trend regarding the employment of the Canadian born children of visible minority immigrants. The author of the report concludes by noting:

> Throughout this report, it has been shown that workers of colour in Canada are experiencing lower incomes, higher unemployment, and persistence in precarious jobs, which all lead to a lower sense of economic security. ... Canadian-born workers of colour, who have higher levels of education than other Canadians in the same age group, are faring worse in comparison to other Canadian workers.[38]

Within the workplace the closing of the wage gap between males and females suffered a serious blow when the Supreme Court of Canada upheld a decision by the Government of Newfoundland and Labrador not to honour on the grounds of financial exigency a wage equity settlement negotiated between the province and a public sector union.[39]

Furthermore, although Canada is one of the first countries in the world to recognize same-sex marriage, something that would have been unthinkable 20 years ago, the ongoing debate over this issue has revealed a new face of discrimination, namely, discrimination between minorities. The debate over same-sex marriage in Canada has brought to the foreground discrimination against members of one minority by members of another. On the other hand, the fact that these debates are occurring marks a significant change from an era in which discrimination was tightly woven into the social fabric, a wrong without a remedy. It would be naïve to say that the creation of the human rights complaints system has eliminated the problem of discrimination. Indeed, it would be far more accurate to say that it has served to bring the extent of the problem more clearly into view. As already noted, numerous reports from human rights commissions and non-governmental agencies have more than amply demonstrated the pervasiveness of race based discrimination in Canada. In addition, we have only scratched the surface of the problem of discrimination against Canadians with disabilities.[40] Nonetheless, it is true that the legal concept of discrimination, the idea that persons who had been discriminated against could seek a remedy at law, did not exist in Canada, or in the international

---

[37] *Racial Status and Employment Outcomes*, online: Canadian Labour Congress <http://canadianlabour.ca/index. php/3/Racial_Status_and_Em>.

[38] *Ibid.*, at 32. The author's linking of discrimination with economic security is especially important.

[39] *Newfoundland (Treasury Board) v. Newfoundland and Labrador Assn. of Public and Private Employees (N.A.P.E.)*, [2004] S.C.J. No. 61, [2004] 3 S.C.R. 381 at para. 98-99.

[40] Handicap and disability are the grounds for by far the largest portion of complaints to human rights commissions, both provincially and federally.

legal order, prior to the Second World War.[41] The fact that discrimination is now all but universally recognized as wrong was one of the major achievements of the second half of the 20th century.[42]

Progress in any area is difficult to measure, in part because of disagreements regarding the standard to be applied. Indeed, the very idea of progress was subject to a great deal of criticism during the 20th century. While the concept had been applied to many areas of human endeavour it had justifiably come to be identified by its critics with the idea of western triumphalism, the superiority of western institutions and the inevitability of their victory over all that had come before. There is, however, a profound difference between believing that progress is possible and simply regarding progress as the inevitable rise of superior societies. It is belief in the inevitability of progress, especially when linked with claims of superiority that should be rejected, not belief in the possibility of progress. Yet, progress, like efficiency, is one of those concepts that is meaningless when taken by itself. There can be no progress without a goal and a measure. In the area of human rights that problem has been addressed because the U.D.H.R. was intended to serve as a "common standard of achievement" against which progress could be measured.

Canada is a state recognized by other states as an independent and sovereign participant in the international community. From the standpoint of international law, as traditionally understood, only states had legal status within the international legal order. The members of the General Assembly of the United Nations who proclaimed the U.D.H.R. in 1948 were representatives of the 56 states who comprised the membership of that body. The U.D.H.R. itself, on the other hand, was addressed to human beings as individuals rather than as representatives of states. In other words, it is not as a citizen or resident of a particular state that every individual is recognized as the bearer of human rights, it is simply as a human being. The U.D.H.R. sets forth "a common standard" that individuals can use to measure the progress of their states toward the achievement of the goals that are set out in its various Articles. It recognizes the right of individuals to hold their states accountable for the failure to promote and protect individual human rights. This means that Canadians, as human beings, can compare the

---

[41] As one would expect, there are scattered antecedents both nationally and internationally. Opposition to discrimination did not emerge all at once.

[42] The primary international human rights instruments dealing explicitly with discrimination are the *International Convention on the Elimination of All Forms of Racial Discrimination* (I.C.E.R.D.), 660 U.N.T.S. 195 (entered into force 4 January 1969, ratified by Canada 14 October 1970) and the *Convention on the Elimination of All Forms of Discrimination Against Women* (C.E.D.A.W.), 1249 U.N.T.S. 13 (entered into force 3 September 1981, ratified by Canada 10 December 1981). Each has been ratified by over 160 countries.

content of Canada's human rights commitments, as evidenced in international agreements, with domestic human rights guarantees. As will become apparent, the vocabulary of human rights within Canada's domestic legal order is but a pale reflection of the rich promise of Canada's international human rights commitments. While many Canadians enjoy much of what the project of human rights is intended to guarantee, they typically do not celebrate this enjoyment in the name of human rights. It is only when the international instruments and the domestic laws are compared that the gulf separating the domestic legal vocabulary from the international commitments becomes apparent. It is hoped that the present selection of international human rights documents and domestic laws will make such comparisons a little easier.

The idea for this collection of human rights materials originated with Philip Petraglia of LexisNexis. It is safe to say that without his encouragement and patience it would never have seen the light of day. Thanks also to Tim Huyer who read a penultimate draft of the introduction and commentary and made a number of valuable suggestions. Some of the text is based upon materials that were originally prepared for the *Canadian Human Rights Act* Review in 1999. I am grateful to the *Department of Justice Canada* for permission to revise those materials for use in the present work.

II.   RECOGNIZING HUMAN RIGHTS

It is often overlooked that the list of Articles in the U.D.H.R. is preceded by the proclamation of a duty rather than a right, namely, the proclamation "that every individual and organ of society, keeping this Declaration constantly in mind, shall strive by teaching and education to promote respect for these rights and freedoms". As the authors of the U.D.H.R. made clear, the key to achieving its goals is education. Not only is there a human right to an education, the human right to an education includes the right to an education in human rights (Article 26). This link is crucial to the success of the project of human rights. Since an education in human rights is both compulsory and universal, human rights language can be understood to provide a common vocabulary, intelligible both to ordinary citizens and to government officials.[43] The human rights project will only succeed if those who are subject to the authority of a government are in a position to remind its officials that they too are bound by the common

---

[43]   For example, see John Humphrey's report of a discussion with Eleanor Roosevelt over the use of "lawyer's language" in the drafting of the U.D.H.R. in John P. Humphrey, *Human Rights and the United Nations: A Great Adventure* (NY: Transnational Publishers, 1984) at 40.

standard of human rights. Governments, after all, are the primary instruments of the project of human wellbeing envisaged by the U.D.H.R. Ordinary citizens, on the other hand, must also be aware that any claims they advance in the name of human rights are claims being made on behalf of all human beings, not just claims made on behalf of themselves or on behalf of groups to which they may belong (Article 1). Those asking government officials for remedies in the name of human rights must be prepared to recognize that they are simultaneously affirming the human rights of everyone else.

An educated citizenry, some of whom may occupy official positions — positions to which everyone has the right of equal access (Article 21) — is the foundation upon which the success of the human rights project ultimately depends. Human rights education bridges the gap between domestic legal and political systems and international human rights standards because the concept of human rights is unintelligible in the absence of references to those standards. Put somewhat more forcefully, the words "human rights", whether used in the context of international law and politics, or in the context of domestic law and politics in any country signatory to the U.D.H.R. simply mean the rights and freedoms set out in the U.D.H.R. and their elaboration in a wide range of human rights treaties. The U.D.H.R. must be the starting point for the project of human rights education. However, this starting point is only available to individuals who are capable of recognizing human rights. Unfortunately, this recognition is often made difficult by the fact that those individuals most accustomed to enjoying the lives envisaged by proponents of human rights are also the least likely to think of those lives in the language of human rights.

Media attention to human rights issues tends to leave the impression that the fight for human rights is a matter of primary concern for those whose rights are not recognized. Television and newspaper images portray the human rights struggle as a struggle by many in other parts of the world for what we in Canada already have: democratic political institutions, rule of law, fundamental freedoms, equality guarantees and social security. In the midst of all of this, the link between what we already have and human rights is rarely made. We are entitled to what we have because we are Canadians, not because we are human. They, whoever they may be, don't have what we have because they are not Canadians. This is their misfortune and we should do something to help, if we can. There is a tendency to believe, however, that it is, first and foremost, their problem. They want to achieve what we have already achieved. Thinking in this way makes it easy to overlook the connection between what we have and human rights. We fail to recognize that if they have human rights to democratic political institutions, rule of law, fundamental freedoms, equality and social security then so do we. When we enjoy these things we do not think of them as being grounded in human rights, we think of them as being grounded in our history and traditions. This is a failure to recognize the place of human rights in our own lives.

Something similar occurs in the coverage of the domestic struggle against various forms of discrimination, the primary focus of human rights attention inside Canada. The fight for equality, the struggle to participate, and the longing for security from want, are the problems of various minorities. Whether they are the disabled, members of visible minorities, gays and lesbians, or the homeless, they stand in need of the help of the majority who may or may not be able or willing to give it to them. Once again, they want what the majority have, but all too often do not recognize as being a matter of human rights. As long as human rights are seen primarily in terms of images of discrimination and abuse the connection between those whose rights are not being recognized, on the one side, and those who fail to recognize the role played by human rights in their own lives, on the other, will be difficult, if not impossible, to make. Those individuals who enjoy what the recognition of human rights is supposed to provide must be made aware of the link between that enjoyment and human rights if they are to take seriously the claims of others for their human rights. Those who abuse human rights cause harm not only to the individuals whose rights they deny but also to the very idea of human rights. The failure to recognize the human rights of one individual is, by the logic of human rights, a failure to recognize the human rights of all individuals. Similarly, those who do not recognize the place of human rights in their own lives harm the idea of human rights by failing to recognize the common ground they share with those whose human rights are not being recognized by others.

There are, therefore, two different ways in which human rights can be recognized. When we speak of states or governments that do not recognize the human rights of their populations we are referring to individuals within those societies who routinely abuse the human rights of other individuals within those societies. It is important to speak of individuals here. Human rights abusers are always individuals, even when, as is typically the case, they act in groups. Institutions do not act, states do not act, governments do not act, except metaphorically. As Christopher Gale and Mark Makarel have noted:

> 'the state' does not violate human rights without the intervention of some human agency, and it is clear that the state must be held responsible for the actions of its own agents and organs, the courts, the police, the armed services, civil servants, etc. when they violate human rights.[44]

---

[44]   Christopher Gane & Mark Mackarel eds., *Human Rights and the Administration of Justice: International Instruments*, (The Hague: Kluwer Law International, 1997) at xxxvi.

It is always individual human beings who act, often in the name of institutions, states, or governments. It is individuals who fail to recognize the human rights of other individuals. The U.D.H.R. places the burden of securing human rights upon "every individual and every organ of society".

Just as it is possible to fail to recognize the human rights of others, it is also possible to fail to recognize one's own human rights. Whenever someone votes in an election (U.D.H.R., Article 21) and doesn't think of this as exercising a human right, that individual reduces the likelihood that he or she will recognize the human right of someone else to vote. Whenever someone calls the police to report a stolen bicycle (Article 17), files a lawsuit (Article 10), endorses a Canada Pension Plan or an Employment Insurance cheque (Articles 22 and 25), writes a letter to the editor or buys a book (Article 19), or attends a church, synagogue or mosque (Article 18) and doesn't recognize that he or she is acting within the domain of human rights, that individual is less likely to identify with the human rights concerns of others. Whenever some individuals in other societies deny these things to other individuals we are quick to recognize these acts as abuses of human rights. Yet, we rarely stop to think that our enjoyment of these same things may also be a matter of human rights. Canadians are not accustomed to thinking of them as human rights because they are not commonly identified as such within the Canadian legal order. However, as Jack Donnelly has written:

> [if] the deepest and broadest attractions of the regimes we most admire arise from their commitment and contribution to human rights, we need to keep human rights in the forefront of the language by which we speak of them.[45]

III. THE INTERNATIONAL BILL OF HUMAN RIGHTS

On June 25, 1993 Canada and 170 other countries marked the conclusion of the World Conference on Human Rights by adopting the *Vienna Declaration and Programme of Action* ("Vienna Declaration").[46] The adoption of the Vienna Declaration was intended to signal a renewed commitment by the signatories to the principles first set forth almost 45 years earlier in the U.D.H.R. The U.D.H.R., proclaimed by the General Assembly of the United Nations on December 10, 1948, was seen by its originators as a call to the conscience of humanity to recognize certain basic standards of human decency. These standards, it was hoped, could be

---

[45] Jack Donnelly, "Human Rights, Democracy, and Development" (1999) 21 Hum. Rts. Q. 610 at 631.

[46] *United Nations World Conference on Human Rights: Vienna Declaration and Programme of Action*, UN Doc. A/CONF. 157/24 (1993).

invoked by subsequent generations in their efforts to prevent a repetition of the horrors that had marked the first half of the 20th century.

The lives of the authors of the U.D.H.R. had been shaped by two major wars, an influenza pandemic, and an economic depression, each of which had been global in scope and impact. They drafted and submitted for approval the text of the U.D.H.R. at the beginning of the Cold War and the onset of the nuclear arms race. The human rights project as originally envisaged was distorted at the outset by the political climate following the Second World War. Over the next four decades the world came to be viewed in terms of a number of oppositions, the most important of which were: the imperial powers and their (soon to be former) colonies; the western powers and the communist states; and the industrially developed societies and those societies defined as being at different stages on the road to industrial development (the presumed destination of all societies around the globe). These differences were also captured in the familiar distinctions between the first world (developed, capitalist, industrial, democratic states), second world (communist/socialist, industrial or industrialising states), third world (states not included in the first two categories), and, most recently, fourth world (aboriginal communities, ethnic groups living within a state or states but lacking the international status of statehood).[47]

The diversity reflected in, but hardly captured by, these categories goes some way toward illustrating the complexity of the human rights project. Membership in the United Nations has more than tripled since 1948 and the alliances that formed the basis of international relations through much of the second half of the 20th century are now defined along different lines. The post-war division between the first and the second worlds was complicated by the fact that the first world was actually further divided into liberal and social democratic states.[48] It was in the political middle ground between the competing economic extremes of free market capitalism and communist central management that the various versions of the social welfare state were constructed. Within the context of debates over these divergent visions of human well-being the unified vision of human rights proclaimed by the General Assembly in 1948 was divided into two parts that were eventually set out in two international covenants: the *International Covenant on Civil and Political Rights*[49] ("I.C.C.P.R.") and the *International Covenant on*

---

[47]   The definitions of these terms are imprecise and, with the end of the Cold War, even more so.

[48]   G. Esping-Andersen, *The Three Worlds of Welfare Capitalism* (Cambridge: Polity Press, 1990). This book contains the most influential, albeit controversial, account of these differences. Esping-Andersen distinguished between social-democratic, corporatist, and liberal versions of "welfare capitalism".

[49]   16 December 1966, 999 U.N.T.S. 171 (entered into force, 23 March 1976).

Economic, Social and Cultural Rights[50] ("I.C.E.S.C.R."). These covenants came into force in 1976. As noted above, Canada is a signatory to both.

Taken together, the U.D.H.R. and the two international covenants make up what is known as the *International Bill of Human Rights*, the foundation document of the international human rights movement. While there are numerous other human rights declarations, covenants and conventions, these three documents retain their primacy as sources of the basic vocabulary of human rights. As their names clearly suggest the two covenants were concerned with different parts, or aspects, of the project, parts whose separation made it possible for states to sign on to those elements within the human rights project that fit most comfortably with that state's own ideology. Thus, the I.C.C.P.R. with it's guarantees of democratic political and legal rights came to be identified with the liberal branch of the human rights project, while the I.C.E.S.C.R. with its emphasis on social welfare and collective rights was characterized as the social democratic, or socialist branch. For example, the United States is a signatory to the I.C.C.P.R. but not to the I.C.E.S.C.R. while China is signatory to the I.C.E.S.C.R., but not to the I.C.C.P.R. It was this division between the two parts of the project that the Vienna Declaration was intended to close.

The intention to reunite the two parts of the original project, while recognizing the diversity of the human community, is most readily apparent in the wording of Article 5 of the Vienna Declaration which reads as follows:

> All human rights are universal, indivisible and interdependent and interrelated. The international community must treat human rights globally in a fair and equal manner, on the same footing, and with the same emphasis. While the significance of national and regional particularities and various historical, cultural and religious backgrounds must be borne in mind, it is the duty of States, regardless of their political, economic and cultural systems, to promote and protect all human rights and fundamental freedoms.[51]

The first sentence of this Article must be understood against the historical background sketched above. In particular, the emphasis placed upon the interdependence and interrelatedness of human rights is intended to re-establish the original vision of the U.D.H.R., a vision in which legal and political rights were not seen as separable from rights to education, health care and social welfare and all human rights and fundamental freedoms were to be enjoyed without discrimination. Thus, since 1993 the international community has recognized the *International Bill of Human Rights*, along

---

[50]   16 December 1966, 993 U.N.T.S. 13 (entered into force, 3 January 1976).
[51]   Vienna Declaration, art. 5.

with a number of related declarations, conventions and covenants, as the source of a shared moral, political and legal vocabulary. Canada is signatory not only to the *International Bill of Human Rights* but also to all of the major human rights instruments.

IV. CANADA'S COMMITMENT TO THE INTERNATIONAL COMMUNITY

At the Summit of World Leaders in September 2005 the United Nations accepted the principle that under certain circumstances the global community has the "responsibility to protect" individual human beings from abuses by their governments. In the *Report of the International Commission on Intervention and State Sovereignty* that set out the foundation for the responsibility to protect, the responsibility was clearly placed within the context of the human rights project:

> 2.16 The adoption of new standards of conduct for states in the protection and advancement of international human rights has been one of the great achievements of the post-World War II era. Article 1.3 of its founding 1945 Charter committed the UN to "promoting and encouraging respect for human rights and for fundamental freedoms for all without distinction as to race, sex, language or religion." The Universal Declaration of Human Rights (1948) embodies the moral code, political consensus and legal synthesis of human rights. The simplicity of the Declaration's language belies the passion of conviction underpinning it. Its elegance has been the font of inspiration down the decades; its provisions comprise the vocabulary of complaint. The two Covenants of 1966, on civil-political and social-economic-cultural rights, affirm and proclaim the human rights norm as a fundamental principle of international relations and add force and specificity to the Universal Declaration.

> 2.17 Together the Universal Declaration and the two Covenants mapped out the international human rights agenda, established the benchmark for state conduct, inspired provisions in many national laws and international conventions, and led to the creation of long-term national infrastructures for the protection and promotion of human rights. They are important milestones in the transition from a culture of violence to a more enlightened culture of peace.[52]

Canada's role in helping to establish recognition of the responsibility to protect was widely seen at the time as consistent with this country's identification with the international human rights movement. Indeed, there is a great deal of evidence available to support the view that Canadian

---

[52] *Report of the International Commission on Intervention and State Sovereignty: The Responsibility to Protect*, September 2001 at 14, online: <http://www. icss.ca/report-en.asp>.

governments have actively fostered the view that Canada is a leader in that movement.

In the 1995 Canadian Foreign Policy review, *Canada in the World*, human rights are identified as central to Canada's role in the international community. Indeed, human rights are listed before democracy and rule of law as a definitive element in the Canadian image abroad. According to the review:

> A priority field of international concern and action for Canadians has been and remains that of human rights. The Government regards respect for human rights not only as a fundamental value, but also as a crucial element in the development of stable, democratic and prosperous societies at peace with each other. From the drafting of the Universal Declaration of Human Rights to that of the recently concluded Convention on the Rights of the Child, we have been in the vanguard of those fighting for international consensus to uphold human freedoms and dignity. We are rightly associated internationally with the promotion of the rights of women and children, and with attention to their role in the economy. Human rights will continue to be a priority for Canada's International Assistance programs.[53]

More recently, in its 2005 International Policy Statement, the Government of Canada reaffirmed Canada's commitment to the human rights project. In the words of the statement:

> Canada is committed to extending human rights and human security throughout the world, a commitment that also forms the foundation of our approach to good governance. ... Although specific governance structures will vary by political and cultural context, Canada's ultimate goal is to foster commitment on human rights, democracy and the rule of law that places individual citizens at the heart of society and creates a state committed to protecting their welfare.[54]

The relationship between this commitment and international treaties is made explicit later in the same policy statement by the Department of Foreign Affairs and International Trade:

> Key to our promotion of the new multilateralism is the strengthening of international human rights institutions. The level of commitment by all countries to the Universal Declaration of Human Rights and other foundation human rights documents is still insufficient.[55]

While numerous other examples of Canada's commitment to the project of human rights could be given, the foregoing will suffice to demonstrate that

---

[53] *Canada in the World: Canadian Foreign Policy Review, 1995*, online: <http://www.international. gc.ca/foreign_policy/cnd-world/chap5-en.asp>.

[54] *A Role of Pride and Influence in the World: Overview*, 2005. Available online at: <http.//geo.international.gc.ca/cip-pic/ipsi/ips-overview5-en.asp>.

[55] *Ibid.*, online at: <http://geo.international.gc.ca/cip-pic/ips/ips-diplomacy7-en.asp>.

those who argue that Canada should make the link between its international human rights commitments and its domestic human rights practices more explicit, are presenting a view that is consistent with Canada's foreign policy.

In pursuit of its commitment to human rights, Canada has established the International Centre for Human Rights and Democratic Development (Rights and Democracy), with a mandate to encourage compliance with the *International Bill of Human Rights*. In the statute creating the Centre its objects are set out in the following terms:

> 4. (1) The objects of the Centre are to initiate, encourage and support cooperation between Canada and other countries in the promotion, development and strengthening of democratic and human rights institutions and programs that give effect to the rights and freedoms enshrined in the *International Bill of Human Rights*, including, among those rights,
>
> (a)   the right to an adequate standard of living;
>
> (b)   the rights of persons not to be subjected to torture or to cruel, inhuman or degrading treatment of punishment;
>
> (c)   the rights of freedom of opinion and expression; and
>
> (d)   the right to vote and be elected at periodic, genuine elections in pluralistic political systems.
>
> (2) A major object of the Centre is to help reduce the wide gap that sometimes exists between the formal adherence of states to international human rights agreements and the actual human rights practices of those states.[56]

The section clearly links rights that are familiar from the Charter (sections 2(b), 3 & 12) with the socio-economic "right to an adequate standard of living". Furthermore, the Centre is dedicated to reducing the "wide gap" that can exist between agreements and practices. At this point there is, of course, no constitutionally protected "right to an adequate standard of living" in Canada.

It is easy to become cynical regarding the gap separating Canada's international commitments and the actions taken by Canadian governments to meet the obligations set out in international human rights agreements. Furthermore, when a representative of the federal Crown is willing to imply in a domestic court that Canada signed treaties like the I.C.C.P.R. "because they created no enforceable obligations", the temptation to be cynical may be

---

[56]   *International Centre for Human Rights and Democratic Development Act*, R.S., 1985, c. 54 (4th Supp.).

difficult to resist.[57] That temptation becomes even stronger when one recognizes that on some matters Canada's domestic policies are diametrically opposed to our international human rights commitments as is the case with increases in university tuition in most provinces. Yet, the temptation should be resisted because the domestic consequences of a human rights treaty must be an act of political will, an expression of the will of the people acting through the instrument of government. The failure to meet fully the obligations of international human rights agreements is a failure of democratic will, not a failure of politicians. It is Canadians who are responsible for ensuring that our international human rights commitments are met, not just Canadian politicians.

As noted earlier, although most Canadians enjoy much of what human rights are intended to guarantee they do not do so in the name of human rights. Within Canada's domestic legal order the phrase "human rights" as it is used in human rights legislation is all but synonymous with the idea of non-discrimination. That there is a human right to non-discrimination is beyond doubt. That this human right is central to the entire human rights project is also beyond doubt. What is too often forgotten is that this right is part of an "interdependent and interrelated" structure of human rights all of which Canada is committed to implementing and protecting. The significance of Article 5 of the Vienna Declaration is that the recognition of one human right requires recognizing all human rights.[58] This is what is meant by the claim that human rights are "interdependent and interrelated". There is no human right in the singular. There are only human rights. The foundation for the articulation of these rights is set out in the *International Bill of Human Rights*. This is the text from which the basic language of human rights must be derived. Any attempt to understand the relation between Canada's international human rights commitments and the place of human rights in the domestic legal order must begin from this text.

---

[57]   *Ahani v. Canada (Minister of Citizenship and Immigration)*, [2002] O.J. No. 431, 58 O.R. 107 (C.A.), Rosenberg J., dissenting at paras. 102-03:

> Counsel for the respondents also seemed to imply that Canada ratified the [International Covenant on Civil and Political Rights] and the [First Optional] Protocol because they created no enforceable obligations. ...

> Counsel argues that if this court were to allow the appellant to wait in Canada for the Committee's views, this would enforce an obligation Canada did not really intend to honour and affect the common understanding of the non-enforceable nature of international treaties. I have already explained why I do not think this is the effect of the protection sought by the appellant. I also find it difficult to accept that the federal government ratified the treaty because it knew it could not be made to comply with its binding obligations. This would undermine the good faith obligation inherent in ratifying treaties. ...

[58]   The significance of this wording of art. 5 is noted on the web site of Foreign Affairs Canada. See: <http://www.dfait-maeci.gc.ca/foreign_policy/human-rights/hr2-rights-en.asp>.

V.   CANADA'S COMPLIANCE: THREE EXAMPLES

Since many people identify the phrase "human rights" with its use in human rights codes it will be useful to consider briefly the actual scope of the idea of human rights in the foundational international agreements. The *International Bill of Human Rights* includes the full range of civil, political, economic, social and cultural rights, as well as the right not to be discriminated against. There are thirty articles in the U.D.H.R. Each of these articles imposes positive obligations upon the people of Canada, not just upon the government, to ensure compliance. Canadians are, however, unaccustomed to employing the vocabulary of human rights when engaging in debates regarding some of the most important issues confronting the country. Three examples, health care, access to higher education, and access to the courts, will suffice to illustrate the gap that separates the meaning of the phrase "human rights" in Canadian law and its meaning in international treaties.

(1) The Right to Health Care

Canadians are justifiably proud of their universal health care system. While the system has been under a good deal of stress in recent years, the majority of Canadians still regard universal access to health care as an essential part of what it means to be Canadian. Few, however, would be inclined to use the language of human rights in this context. Yet, Article 25(1) of the U.D.H.R. reads as follows:

> Everyone has the right to a standard of living adequate for the health and well-being of himself and of his family, including food, clothing, housing and medical care and necessary social services, and the right to security in the event of unemployment, sickness, disability, widowhood, old age or other lack of livelihood in circumstances beyond his control.[59]

The promise held out by Article 25(1) clearly requires a commitment on the part of the community to ensure a basic level of socio-economic well being for every member. Articles 11 and 12 of the I.C.E.S.C.R. elaborate on this promise by setting out in greater detail what is required to fulfill it. For example, Article 12(2)(d) imposes an obligation upon the state's population to ensure:

---

[59]   U.D.H.R., art. 25(1).

> The creation of conditions which would assure to all medical service and
> medical attention in the event of sickness.[60]

It is readily apparent that the Canadian Medicare system could be viewed as
a fulfillment of the obligation assumed by Canadians under Article 12 of the
I.C.E.S.C.R.[61] There is, however, no reference to human rights in the
Canada Health Act[62] nor in the various provincial health insurance statutes.
While the *Canada Health Act* sets out a commitment to the five principles of
universal access to health care, no reference is made to the existence, clearly
set out in treaties ratified by Canada, to Article 25 of the U.D.H.R. or Article
12 of the I.C.E.S.C.R. Furthermore, the *Canada Health Act* and the various
provincial statutes are subject to repeal or amendment at any time. Since the
courts have held that there is no constitutionally protected right to health
care, only the right to have whatever services governments choose to
provide delivered in a non-discriminatory fashion, the protection of the
human right to access to health care falls far short of what is required by
Article 12(2)(d).[63]

(2) The Right to a Higher Education

One of the more interesting illustrations of the gap separating Canada's
domestic policies from its international human rights obligations can be
found in the ongoing debate over access to post-secondary education. Article
26 of the U.D.H.R. guarantees everyone a right to an education. This right is
defined more fully in Article 13 of the I.C.E.S.C.R. In particular, Article
13(2)(c) guarantees:

> Higher education shall be made equally accessible to all, on the basis of
> capacity, by every appropriate means, and in particular by the progressive
> introduction of free education;[64]

---

[60] I.C.E.S.C.R., art. 12(2)(d).

[61] In the *Fifth Periodic Report on the Implementation of the International Covenant on Economic,
Social and Cultural Rights*, submitted to the Committee on Economic, Social and Cultural
Rights, the Government of Canada noted (at 12) that:

> Federal, provincial, and territorial governments continue to collaborate on many health
> and social programming initiatives that serve to implement the provisions of the
> *International Covenant on Economic, Social, and Cultural Rights*.

Available online at: <http://www.unhchr.ch/tbs/doc.nsf/898586b1dc7b4043c1256a450044f331/
4f07de4ea236e858c125711500574ff8/$FILE/G0543784.pdf>.

[62] R.S., 1985, c. C-6.

[63] *Auton (Guardian ad litem of) v. British Columbia (Attorney General)*, [2004] S.C.J. No. 71,
[2004] 3 S.C.R. 657 at para. 41.

[64] I.C.E.S.C.R., art. 13(2)(c).

In most parts of Canada the cost of post-secondary education has dramatically increased over the past 10 years. In a recent report on post-secondary education in the Province of Ontario it was noted that "people have a right to develop to their full potential".[65] This is similar to the wording of the U.D.H.R. and the I.C.E.S.C.R. which refer to the "right to the full development of the human personality". There is, however, nothing in the report to suggest the link between the human right to an education and the reform of post-secondary education in Ontario. While the report uses the terms "higher education" and "postsecondary education" interchangeably, and the possibility of eliminating tuition is briefly addressed, there is no reference in these passages to the idea that access to higher education for qualified individuals should be guaranteed as a human right.[66] There is, as one would expect, reference to the Ontario *Human Rights Code* in the report but this occurs in the context of recommendations regarding increased access for persons with disabilities to post-secondary education.[67] The argument in support of these recommendations, like those in support of any attempt to improve access, would clearly be strengthened if it was made in a context in which the human right to higher education was being affirmed. It is precisely because there is such a human right that access to higher education should be guaranteed to all qualified individuals without discrimination.

(3)   The Right of Access to an Independent and Impartial Judiciary

Unlike health care and education, an independent and impartial judiciary is constitutionally protected in Canada. However, as conceived by the courts the Constitution protects the institution rather than guaranteeing a right of access to the courts on the part of Canadians. Like universal health care and higher education, access to justice has not been conceived as a human right within the Canadian legal order. While there are a number of Articles in the U.D.H.R. and the covenants dealing with the judiciary, Article 10 of the U.D.H.R. is the most straightforward guarantee of access to an independent and impartial judiciary. The Article reads in full:

---

[65]   *Ontario: A Leader in Learning, Report and Recommendations*, (Toronto: Queen's Printer, 2005) at 6, online: <http://www.edu.gov.on.ca/eng/document/reports/postsec.pdf>.
[66]   *Ibid.*, at 23.
[67]   *Ibid.*, 32, 68ff. *Human Rights Code*, R.S.O. 1990, c. H.19.

> Everyone is entitled in full equality to a fair and public hearing by an independent and impartial tribunal, in the determination of his rights and obligations and of any criminal charge against him.[68]

The implications of this particular guarantee are developed more fully in Article 14 of the I.C.C.P.R. The first two sentences of this Article set out in greater detail the meaning of Article 10:

> All persons shall be equal before the courts and tribunals. In the determination of any criminal charge against him, or of his rights and obligations in a suit at law, everyone shall be entitled to a fair and public hearing by a competent, independent and impartial tribunal established by law.[69]

Canadians, therefore, have a human right of access to an independent and impartial adjudication of their rights, a right deriving from these Articles. It should be noted that both Article 10 of the U.D.H.R. and Article 14 of the I.C.C.P.R. refer to both the criminal and the civil courts.

It could be argued, of course, that as long as Canadians enjoy universal health care, access to schools and an independent and impartial judiciary it doesn't matter that they are not identified with the project of human rights. For the individual awaiting treatment, applying to a college or university, or about to stand trial the fact that there is a human right to access will likely seem far less important than the access itself. Yet, there is much more at stake here than a concern with a name. By not characterizing access to health care, education and the courts as human rights, they are removed from the domain of demands that individual Canadians might make against their state, demands justified on the basis of commitments made by Canada to the international community. While the independence and impartiality of the judiciary may be guaranteed by the Canadian Constitution, access to the judiciary is not. For example, an individual lacking the resources to bring an action before a Canadian court has no constitutionally protected right of access. Similarly, Canada's health care system rests upon a complex set of interlocking federal and provincial statutes, none of which enjoys the status of quasi-constitutional law conferred upon anti-discrimination statutes, let alone being constitutionally protected.

With a few limited exceptions, including the *Canadian Bill of Rights* and some provincial statutes, human rights legislation in Canada is largely concerned with equality of opportunity and the prohibition of discrimination.[70] While these statutes are clearly central to the project of

---

[68]   U.D.H.R., art. 10.

[69]   I.C.C.P.R., art. 14.

[70]   Like the *Bill of Rights*, a number of provincial human rights statutes include rights and freedoms in addition to the right not to be discriminated against. For example, the Quebec *Charter of*

human rights, international human rights agreements consistently link anti-discrimination laws with the broader project of human rights implementation and protection. The rights guaranteeing access to health care, education and an independent and impartial judiciary are to be ensured and protected in a non-discriminatory fashion. In addition, the right not to be discriminated against is one human right among others. Article 5 of the Vienna Declaration clearly links that right to all of the others. Human rights statutes that use the phrase in a more restricted sense serve only to obscure the connection between the language of Canada's international human rights commitments and the domestic environment in which those commitments are to be met.

VI. DISCRIMINATION AND HUMAN RIGHTS

While the *Charter of Rights and Freedoms* entrenches a number of human rights in the Canadian Constitution it does not do so in the name of human rights. With the exception of the right to property, those rights that are called human rights in the *Canadian Bill of Rights* have largely been superceded by the Charter. As noted above the phrase "human rights protection" in Canada, in the federal as well as the provincial and territorial jurisdictions, typically refers to statutes dealing with the right not to be discriminated against. There is a human right (or complex of rights) to non-discrimination (U.D.H.R., Articles 2 & 7) as well as a human right to a process that includes the possibility of an independent and impartial adjudication of the complaint (U.D.H.R., Article 7). Yet, although the preambles to some provincial and territorial human rights codes include references to the U.D.H.R., none of them is clearly stated to be implementing any part of Canada's international human rights commitments. Furthermore, the phrase "human rights" typically does not occur in the statutory provisions themselves. Strictly speaking it would make more sense to speak of a anti-discrimination legislation than of human rights legislation.[71] It is important to understand what this means.

While Canada provides statutory (quasi-constitutional) and constitutional protection against discrimination, there is a distinction between having access to a complaints process that includes the possibility of adjudication and having a recognized human right to such access. Like all human rights the right to non-discrimination, which includes the right to a

---

Human Rights and Freedoms extends the concept of human rights protection much further than is typically the case with human rights legislation (*Charter of Human Rights and Freedoms*, R.S.Q., c. C-12).

[71] Although both phrases are used, Canadian courts use the phrase "human rights legislation" with much greater frequency than the phrase "anti-discrimination legislation".

non-discrimination jurisdiction for dealing with complaints of discrimination, is not a free standing right. Moreover, there are two different senses in which this is true of the right to non-discrimination. First, the human right to non-discrimination is actually dependent upon the existence of other rights because it is in the pursuit of those rights that discrimination occurs. In other words, the right to non-discrimination requires that other rights claims, not only human, but also constitutional and statutory, be dealt with without discrimination on the basis of a variety of prohibited grounds. The latter two types of rights, which may not themselves be clearly identified as human rights, are, nonetheless, subject to the principle of non-discrimination. To be discriminated against is to be denied something to which one has a right. This is why it would not be going too far to say that at this point in time the right to non-discrimination is the only widely recognized human right in Canada insofar as it is the only right which is typically explicitly labeled as such.

Second, as already noted, the interconnectedness of human rights means that the human right not to be discriminated against cannot be separated from the complex of human rights set out in the international agreements. Labeling the right to non-discrimination a "human right", which is to say a universal right, rather than just a constitutional or a statutory right, (*ie.*, rights which are not universal), has the effect of raising the question of the existence of other recognized human rights, that is to say, other human rights that could be incorporated into the domestic legal order in such a way that they too could be claimed. While section 1 of the *Canadian Bill of Rights* actually identifies six human rights that are linked to the principle of non-discrimination, neither the *Charter of Rights and Freedoms* nor most human rights legislation make any reference to specific human rights.

At this point in Canadian history the only human right that can be said to be widely recognized as a part of Canada's domestic legal system under the name of human rights is the right to non-discrimination. The centrality of the opposition to discrimination to the human rights movement is evident in the *Charter of the United Nations* where the content of the concept of human rights is largely confined to the idea of prohibiting discrimination on the basis of "race, sex, language, or religion".[72] Taken by itself this might be seen as lending weight to the argument that the identification of the domestic human rights project in Canada, with the elimination of discrimination, is consistent with the international concept of human rights. Such a view is inconsistent, however, not only with the concept of discrimination in the U.D.H.R., but also with the definition of "discrimination" in the two major

---

[72]   Johannes Morsink, *The Universal Declaration of Human Rights: Origins, Drafting and Intent* (Philadelphia: University of Pennsylvania Press, 1999) at 92.

human rights conventions that deal explicitly with the problem of discrimination, *ie.*, the *International Convention on the Elimination of All Forms of Racial Discrimination*[73] ("C.E.R.D.") and *Convention on the Elimination of All Forms of Discrimination against Women*[74] ("C.E.D.A.W.") (as well as the I.C.E.S.C.R. and the I.C.C.P.R).

While the word "discrimination" is not used, Article 2 of the U.D.H.R. introduces the concept of discrimination, understood as drawing a distinction on a prohibited ground, with explicit reference to the underlying rights and freedoms guaranteed in the U.D.H.R. The first part of the Article reads as follows:

> Everyone is entitled to all the rights and freedoms set forth in this Declaration, without distinction of any kind, such as race, colour, sex, language, religion, political or other opinion, national or social origin, property, birth or other status.[75]

According to this Article the rights and freedoms are primary and their fulfillment and protection is not to be withheld on the basis of irrelevant considerations such as those listed in the text of the Article. The word "discrimination" itself does not occur until Article 7 of the U.D.H.R. which reads:

> All are equal before the law and are entitled without any discrimination to equal protection of the law. All are entitled to equal protection against any discrimination in violation of this Declaration and against any incitement to such discrimination.[76]

It is assumed in this Article that the meaning of "discrimination" does not require a definition. The link between the grounds of discrimination and equality before the law is made explicit in Article 26 of the I.C.C.P.R.:

> All persons are equal before the law and are entitled without any discrimination to the equal protection of the law. In this respect, the law shall prohibit any discrimination and guarantee to all persons equal and effective protection against discrimination on any ground such as race, colour, sex, language, religion, political or other opinion, national or social origin, property, birth or other status.[77]

Although no laws in Canada make explicit reference to this Article, human rights legislation and section 15(1) of the *Charter of Rights and Freedoms* can be seen as an attempt within the domestic legal order to meet this requirement. However, as noted earlier no Canadian laws explicitly

---

[73]   660 U.N.T.S. 195, entered into force 4 January 1969.
[74]   1249 U.N.T.S. 513, entered into force 3 September 1981.
[75]   U.D.H.R., art. 2.
[76]   U.D.H.R., art. 7.
[77]   I.C.C.P.R., art. 26.

implement Canada's international human rights commitments, although the preambles of some human rights codes make reference to the U.D.H.R.

In addition to the clear connection between underlying rights and discrimination in the U.D.H.R. both of the international covenants contain Articles in which this link is set out. Article 2(1) of the I.C.C.P.R. reads:

> Each State Party to the present Covenant undertakes to respect and to ensure to all individuals within its territory and subject to its jurisdiction the rights recognized in the present Covenant, without distinction of any kind, such as race, colour, sex, language, religion, political or other opinion, national or social origin, property, birth or other status.[78]

Similarly, Article 2(2) of the I.C.E.S.C.R. reads:

> The States Parties to the present Covenant undertake to guarantee that the rights enunciated in the present Covenant will be exercised without discrimination of any kind as to race, colour, sex, language, religion, political or other opinion, national or social origin, property, birth or other status.[79]

Furthermore, the two conventions that deal with specific grounds of discrimination, (*i.e.*, race and sex), also clearly link the concept to the underlying guarantee of the rights and freedoms that signatories to the conventions are committed to ensuring and protecting. Article 1 of C.E.R.D. reads:

> In this Convention, the term "racial discrimination" shall mean any distinction, exclusion, restriction or preference based on race, colour, descent, or national or ethnic origin which has the purpose or effect of nullifying or impairing the recognition, enjoyment or exercise, on an equal footing, of human rights and fundamental freedoms in the political, economic, social, cultural or any other field of public life.[80]

The same connection is evident in Article 1 of C.E.D.A.W.:

> For the purposes of the present Convention, the term "discrimination against women" shall mean any distinction, exclusion or restriction made on the basis of sex which has the effect or purpose of impairing or nullifying the recognition, enjoyment or exercise by women, irrespective of their marital status, on a basis of equality of men and women, of human rights and fundamental freedoms in the political, economic, social, cultural, civil or any other field.[81]

Finally, in the more recent *Convention on the Rights of the Child*, Article 2 reads:

---

[78] I.C.C.P.R., art. 2(1).
[79] I.C.E.S.C.R, art. 2(2).
[80] C.E.R.D., art. 1.
[81] C.E.D.A.W., art. 1.

> States Parties shall respect and ensure the rights set forth in the present
> Convention to each child within their jurisdiction without discrimination of
> any kind, irrespective of the child's or his or her parent's or legal guardian's
> race, colour, sex, language, religion, political or other opinion, national,
> ethnic or social origin, property, disability, birth or other status.[82]

Canada is signatory to all of these conventions although no Canadian law makes explicit reference to any of them.

It is readily apparent on the basis of the foregoing that within the international legal order the concept of discrimination is inextricably linked to the fundamental rights and freedoms guaranteed by the U.D.H.R. While there is a right not to be discriminated against, calling that right a "human right" immediately brings into view the rest of the human rights project. The fact that Canada is signatory to all of these agreements means that Canadians are committed to creating a social, political, and legal order in which this connection is explicitly recognized. This would require making the connection between the right not to be discriminated against and human rights explicit. Doing so would make the link between that human right and all other human rights part of the legal order through the implementation of Canada's international agreements in domestic law.

VII. THE UNIVERSALITY OF HUMAN RIGHTS

In signing the U.D.H.R. representatives of Canada committed Canadians as well as all other human beings around the world, to a common set of moral principles. It is a sign of the power of these principles that no serious Canadian politician at the beginning of the 21st century could stand in opposition to the idea of human rights. The ratification of the international covenants and a number of other treaties imposed political and legal obligations upon Canadians based upon this set of universal values. As a call to the reason and conscience of individual human beings the U.D.H.R. appears to rest upon the presumption that everyone accepts the rights set out within it. However, since it is not true that all human beings are persuaded by its claims, supporters of the U.D.H.R. are potentially placed in the position of imposing its values upon others who do not accept them. In this way the U.D.H.R. threatens to become the basis of yet another authoritarian ideology, a point of view intolerant of those with competing points of view. It is incumbent upon those who would proclaim and defend human rights to

---

[82]   *Convention on the Rights of the Child*, G.A. Res. 44/25, A/Res/44/25 (1989), (entered into force 2 September, 1990).

answer such objections, to show how the offer of equality provides a more secure foundation for human well being than the presumption of superiority.

Anyone embarking upon the study of human rights would do well, therefore, to reflect upon the opening sentence of Article 1 of the U.D.H.R.:

> All human beings are born free and equal in dignity and rights.

While this sentence reads like a straightforward statement of an obvious truth, it is actually at odds with the beliefs of most human beings throughout most of human history. Many societies throughout history have practised some form of slavery. Enslavement was widely practised in Europe and in Asia as recently as the Second World War. Debt bondage, a relationship all but indistinguishable from slavery, continues to be practised in parts of the world today.[83] While being born into slavery may not be as common as being enslaved as a child or an adult, it is nonetheless true that institutionalised slavery has played a large part in the history of human societies around the world. Many human beings throughout history have not been born free. Similarly, aristocratic societies in which demarcations in social status were determined at birth have been the norm rather than the exception. The idea that some individuals are superior to others by virtue of the circumstances of their birth would certainly not have been alien to the minds of the vast majority of our predecessors. Undoubtedly there are still those today who believe that their birth marked their entry into a superior class of human beings. Again, throughout much of human history, few have believed that all human beings were born equal in dignity. Finally, differences in political and civil rights have also been the norm throughout the world at most times and places. It wasn't until the 19th century that the ideal of a universal franchise began to be realised, and in many parts of the world today voting rights are restricted or non-existent. Women and members of religious and ethnic minorities remain second class citizens in many countries. Thus, the idea that human beings are equal in rights marks a radical departure from common historical practices. The sentence, therefore, is not a simple statement of fact. Nor, for that matter, is it a statement of a universally held belief. Large numbers of human beings in the contemporary world continue to believe that the circumstances of their birth provide the basis for entitlements.

The concept of "equality" is notoriously difficult to define. Indeed, it often seems easier to say what it isn't than to state clearly what it is. It is important, therefore, to be very careful in defining what Article 1 actually

---

[83]   While "legal slavery" has been universally abolished the practice of *de facto* slavery continues in many countries around the world. Kevin Bales notes that household slaves exist in Paris, London, New York, Zurich and Los Angeles (*Disposable People: New Slavery in the Global Economy*, rev. ed. (Berkeley: University of California Press, 2004) at 3).

says. It does not state "All human beings are born free and equal", it affirms that:

> All human beings are born free and *equal in dignity and rights*. [Emphasis added.]

The first part of the Article affirms that no one is born the property of another; as such it is an explicit denial of the moral possibility of slavery. This part of the affirmation is unqualified. It is the notion of equality that is qualified by the phrase "in dignity and rights". When dignity is understood as a name for moral worth, "equal in dignity" means that no human being is born morally superior to any other human being. Finally, "equal in rights" means equal with regard to the rights set out in the U.D.H.R., *ie.*, human rights.

The following passage from one of Norberto Bobbio's last works sets out a useful approach to defining "equality", an approach that is particularly sensitive to the various contexts in which the idea must be given a practical sense. Bobbio wrote:

> The concept of equality is relative, not absolute. It is relative to at least three variables which have to be taken into account every time the desirability of equality or its practicability are discussed: (a) the individuals between whom benefits and obligations should be shared; (b) the benefits or obligations to be shared; (c) the criteria by which they should be shared.[84]

Two examples will illustrate the usefulness of this model for understanding the meaning of equality in the context of human rights. The universality of human rights means that the first variable includes all human beings. If the second variable is health care then the third variable, the appropriate criterion, will be need. Thus, all human beings have a right to health care on the basis of need. If the second variable is education, then the third variable will be merit. All human beings have a right to an education suited to their demonstrated abilities. It doesn't follow from this that all human beings have a right to the *same* health care or to the *same* education. There are numerous contextual factors that would have to be taken into account by policymakers attempting to ensure compliance with the obligation to provide health care and education on the basis of the appropriate criterion. Nonetheless, Bobbio's set of variables provides guidance for those designing health care and educational institutions by, for example, highlighting the fact that differences in wealth or social status are morally irrelevant criteria when it comes to deciding who should have access to hospitals and schools.

---

[84] Norberto Bobbio, *Left and Right: The Significance of a Political Distinction*, trans. by Allan Cameron (Cambridge: Polity Press, 1996) at 60.

Whatever its precise definition, the concept of "human equality" belongs first of all to the vocabulary of morality, where it is grounded in the recognition of the moral neutrality of the universal human fact of birth.[85] No one deserves the circumstances of their birth and for this reason alone no just social order, domestic or international, can be grounded in distinctions drawn among the newly born. Understood in this way, equality is intended to serve both as the foundation of legal and political institutions, wherein it finds its most concrete expression, and as the measure of legal and political behaviour within those institutions. The project of defining "human equality" is, therefore, a legal and a political project, not just an intellectual exercise. It is a project in which all human beings, simply by virtue of their humanity, are entitled to participate.[86] While there are precedents to the idea of the universal moral worth of human beings, the U.D.H.R. marks the first serious attempt in human history to create political, legal and social welfare institutions whose legitimacy rests solely upon that claim.

The opening sentence of Article 1 sets the stage for all that follows. Although it is not written as a set of laws, the U.D.H.R. was intended by the signatories to provide the basis for the drafting of legal documents at both the international and the national level. This interlocking set of treaties, constitutions and legislation was intended to provide the legal framework necessary for the promotion and protection of human rights at the domestic level. The primary instruments of that promotion and protection were to be the governments of the signatory states themselves. It was the states who would make the commitments to other states within the international legal order. It was those same states who would then make good on those commitments through the structuring of their domestic legal systems. As subsequent developments have shown this dual role has proven to be the weakest point in the entire project. International agreements are routinely signed by states that have no intention of implementing them through domestic legislation. This is as true of states whose citizens enjoy much of what the human rights project was intended to guarantee, as it is of states whose citizens don't. Recognizing human rights requires using the vocabulary of human rights not only in the context of international relations but also within domestic legal orders where the full implications of that recognition for individuals are intended to be developed. What precisely

---

[85]   This claim will not strike everyone as culturally neutral. Religious traditions which include the idea of reincarnation or of original sin are clearly at odds with the notion that birth, in and of itself, carries no moral consequences.

[86]   Norberto Bobbio, *The Age of Rights*, Trans. Allan Cameron (Cambridge: Polity Press, 1996) at 13:
    The *Universal Declaration of Human Rights* represents a unique demonstration that a value system can be considered to be founded on humanity and thus acknowledged by it: the proof is in the general consensus over its validity.

does this mean? Before examining the significance of the *International Bill of Human Rights* within Canada's domestic legal order it will be helpful to briefly consider some of the current debates centered on the basic concept of human rights.

VIII. THE MEANING OF HUMAN RIGHTS: SOME ONGOING DEBATES

One of the major difficulties confronting the student of human rights is the range of debates regarding the meaning of the term, debates that are at once moral, political, historical and legal. In addition to debates regarding the meaning to be given to such basic terms as "universal" and "equality", there are numerous controversies involving the meaning of the very concept of a human right. As a result there is a real potential for confusion deriving from the terminology in which these debates are conducted.[87] Participants in these debates speak of generations of rights, negative and positive rights, minority and group rights and competing culturally based models of human rights. It would not be surprising, therefore, if those approaching the field of human rights for the first time concluded that no one really knows what human rights are. This is unfortunate because the concept of human rights is actually relatively straightforward. No one would argue that it follows from the fact that there are debates over the interpretation of the meanings of particular laws, or over the concept of law itself, that there are no laws. Similarly, it does not follow from the fact that there are debates over the meaning of particular rights, or over the concept of human rights, that there are no human rights. The problems with the concept derive not so much from the difficulty in saying what human rights are, as they derive from the practical obstacles that stand in the way of their implementation. Nonetheless, in the context of these various controversies the vocabulary of human rights can appear intimidating. The following sections are intended to briefly address some of the major issues at the heart of ongoing debates regarding human rights beginning with a brief consideration of what it means to say that there are human rights.

---

[87]   This problem is further complicated by the diversity of academic disciplines within which discussions regarding human rights occur. In spite of the emphasis upon interdisciplinarity in the past decades (or perhaps because of it) lawyers, political scientists and philosophers do not always speak the same language when it comes to discussing human rights.

(1) The Existence of Human Rights

It is a legal fact in the history of the Canadian constitutional order that Canada has recognized human rights. The academic debate over whether or not there are human rights was resolved in Canada by the signing of the U.D.H.R. and by the ratification of the I.C.E.S.C.R. and the I.C.C.P.R. Within the legal and political order of Canada it is as pointless to debate the existence of human rights as it would be to debate the existence of Canadian laws. While there is room to debate the significance of human rights within the Canadian legal order, any account of Canadian law which neglects to include both the existence of human rights and the recognition of those rights is, for that reason alone, incomplete. This means that debates over human rights policy must focus upon the question of implementing Canada's human rights obligations rather than upon the deeper question of whether or not Canada has such obligations. We could live in a world that did not recognize human rights, just as we could live in a world without laws. The simple fact of the matter is that we do not. As the philosopher Richard Rorty has noted, the existence of human rights is an institutional fact in the contemporary world.[88]

(2) Human Rights and Human Duties

It is often said that participants in the human rights movement talk about rights while ignoring the equally important domain of human duties and responsibilities. This may be the most commonly misunderstood feature of the concept of human rights. As already noted, the U.D.H.R. begins with the duty placed upon "every individual and organ of society" to "strive by teaching and education to promote respect for (the) rights and freedoms" that follow. In addition, Article 29(1), the second last article, also imposes duties toward the community in which one lives. Indeed, the concept of duty is central to the very idea of human rights. Unlike the use of the notions of rights and duties in other contexts, where the possession of a right implies the existence of someone else with a duty, the concept of a human right also includes the duty to recognize that right in all other human beings. By claiming something as a human right one is simultaneously assuming the duty to recognize the claims of others to the same right. For example, if one invokes the right to freedom of thought, conscience and religion guaranteed

---

[88] Richard Rorty, "Human Rights, Rationality, and Sentimentality" in Stephen Shute & Susan Hurley, eds., *On Human Rights: The Oxford Amnesty Lectures 1993*, (New York: Basic Books, 1993) at 111, 116, 134.

under Article 18 of the U.D.H.R. then one is also taking on the duty to respect that same human right in everyone else.

While it is true that there can be no meaningful human right without the duty of others to recognize that right, it is equally true that any claim to a human right necessarily imposes the duty upon the claimant to recognize and respect that same right in every other human being. It is here that the distinction drawn earlier between the two senses of recognizing human rights is significant. Whenever I recognize something as a human right that I possess, I simultaneously assume a duty to recognize that right in every other human being. This duty is the moral content of the concept of a human right, not the right itself. If I am unprepared to recognize the same right in every other human being then I have failed to advance a meaningful claim to a human right on my own behalf. The emphasis on rights over duties results, in part, from the fact noted earlier that attention to human rights tends to focus upon the lives of those whose rights are being denied rather than upon those who are enjoying their benefits.

(3)   Human Rights and Cultural Values

The debate surrounding both the Bangkok and the Tunis Declarations raised the question of whether there are differences among human rights in different cultural traditions.[89] There is, however, a crucial difference between claiming that human rights mean different things in different cultures and saying that different cultures may find different ways of giving expression to the same basic rights. With the first alternative there are no universal human rights and it would be better to stop talking about them. With the second alternative there are universal human rights but these same rights can take different institutional forms in accordance with the different traditions in which they find expression.[90] This latter alternative was reinforced in the Vienna Declaration, a statement which makes it clear that human rights are an either/or: *either* there are rights possessed by every human being by virtue of the simple fact that they are human *or* there are no

---

[89]   "Bangkok Declaration" (1993) 14 H.R.L.J. 370, "Tunis Declaration" (1993) 14 H.R.L.J. 367.

[90]   Radhika Coomaraswamy, comments on Shmuel N. Eisenstadt, "Human Rights in Comparative Civilizational Perspective", in Asbjørn Eide & Bernt Hagtvet eds., *Human Rights in Perspective: A Global Assessment*, (Oxford: Blackwell, 1992) at 247:

    I must also add that I do not accept the premise ... that the human rights idea is Western. The legal and political institutions may be, but the idea has been articulated in Asian societies long before - one needs only to look at the edicts of King Asoka.

human rights. To speak of human rights possessed only by this or that group of human beings is no longer to speak the language of human rights.[91]

The argument in favour of culturally specific human rights is commonly paired with the argument that human rights themselves are the product of European or Western traditions and are, therefore, culturally specific. While the Second World War provided the immediate historical context for the drafting of the U.D.H.R., it is against the much longer historical background of the idea that there are degrees of humanity, that some human beings have a natural right to exercise power over others, that the language of the U.D.H.R. must be interpreted. The revolutions of 1688 in England, 1776 in the United States and 1789 in France may all be understood as partial rejections of the political legitimacy of this distinction in "the West". However, each of these events left various forms of inequality deeply entrenched within the resulting legal orders, that is to say, within European or Western cultural traditions. Furthermore, in each and every case these battles for rights were fought against others who claimed, with justification, to represent European or Western traditions.[92] This fact cannot be emphasized too much. The battle for the recognition of universal rights within the Western tradition was, and continues to be, fought against opponents within that same tradition, opponents who argue that human rights are not consistent with the core cultural and religious values of the West. Unless this is continually affirmed, then those fighting for human rights within other traditions will be identified as the importers of Western values, rather than as the companions of those who have fought, and continue to fight, for the recognition of human rights within the West itself.

---

[91] That the authors of the U.D.H.R. were fully aware of this has been well demonstrated by Johannes Morsink, *The Universal Declaration of Human Rights: Origins, Drafting and Intent* (Philadelphia: University of Pennsylvania Press, 1999) at 281-328. Similarly, Paul Gordon Lauren points to antecedents of the basic ideas underlying the U.D.H.R. in a number of different cultural and religious traditions in *The Evolution of International Human Rights: Visions Seen* (Philadelphia: University of Pennsylvania Press, 1998), at 4-36. As the international human rights movement continues to spread, it is likely that precursors of its fundamental values will be found in many of the world's major cultural and religious traditions.

[92] There were outspoken opponents of the idea of universal rights even among those who were reformers. For example, Jeremy Bentham noted that among other flaws in the *Declaration of Rights* passed by the French National Assembly in 1791, the claims that "all men are born free" and that "all men are born equal in rights" were "notoriously and undeniably false" (Jeremy Bentham, "Nonsense Upon Stilts, or Pandora's Box Opened, or the French Declaration of Rights Prefixed to the Constitution of 1791 Laid Open and Exposed — With a Comparative Sketch of What has been Done on the Same Subject in the Constitution of 1795, and a Sample of Citizen Sieyes" in Philip Schofield, Catherine Pease-Watkin, & Cyprian Blamires, eds., *Rights, Representation, and Reform: Nonsense Upon Stilts and Other Writings on the French Revolution* (Oxford: Clarendon, 2002) at 323).

If the Enlightenment stands for anything at all it marks the repudiation of the Western idea that there is a natural hierarchy among human beings that can be used to justify the exercise of political power by one group of human beings over another. This is not to say, of course, that ancient Western traditions of natural privilege and entitlement, often supported by religious doctrines, all came to an abrupt halt in the 18th century.[93] On the contrary, the age of European imperialism reached its peak in the century following the Enlightenment and the defenders of imperialism regularly invoked the idea of a natural hierarchy in justification of the practice of colonialism.[94] Furthermore, the historical fact that European imperialism flourished in the wake of the great declarations of human rights in the 18th century has done grave damage to the project of human rights in the eyes of much of the modern world.[95] Yet, when allowances are made for historical context, it is clear that the target of the great 18th century proponents of universal rights was the predecessor tradition of natural inequality within Europe itself. This tradition had been used to justify slavery and the exclusion of women from public life, as well as colonialism.[96] Those who would defend natural inequalities elsewhere in the modern world on the ground that the idea that human beings are possessed of equal human rights is Eurocentric, routinely neglect this aspect of the historical background of the human rights movement.[97] It is a fact of history that the modern

---

[93]   Michael J. Perry, "Are Human Rights Universal? The Relativist Challenge and Related Matters" (1997) 19 Hum. Rts. Q. 461 at 464:
    Cast as the claim that only some persons are human beings, the claim that only some human beings are sacred has been, and remains quite common.

[94]   V.G. Kiernan, The Lords of Human Kind: European Attitudes toward the outside world in the Imperial Age (London: Weidenfield and Nicolson, 1969) at 312:
    At home Europe was shuffling away from forms of society based on compulsion towards new ones founded on assent. Abroad it was acting in the opposite spirit.

[95]   The consequences of this history are clearly evident in the tension between the rights guaranteed in the U.D.H.R., rights expressed in terms of individuals, and the opening Articles of the I.C.E.S.C.R. and the I.C.C.P.R. with their references to the self-determination of peoples.

[96]   The most widely influential argument for natural slavery and the inferiority of women was, of course, presented by Aristotle in Book I of his Politics. One of the more significant debates over the authority of Aristotle on the matter of natural slavery was held in the Spanish university town of Valladolid in 1550 between Bartolomé de las Casas and Juan Ginés de Sepúlveda. The latter maintained that the inhabitants of the New World were natural slaves in Aristotle's sense while the former, who had actually lived among them, argued for their common humanity, albeit with the goal of converting them to Christianity. For an account of the debate and of the role of Aristotle's view of slavery see Lewis Hanke, Aristotle and the American Indians: A Study in Race Prejudice in the Modern World (Bloomington: Indiana University Press, 1959) at 14-18, 44-61.

[97]   The historical fact that many of the often cited forerunners of modern human rights texts were written by European males is more a reflection of the context in which they were written, than it is a basis for judging the consequences of their having been written. While the rejection of the principle of natural inequality may have been originally articulated largely in terms of relations among certain groups of male property owners (who created a "natural right" to property in the

movement toward the recognition of universal rights was born in Europe but it is systematically misleading to characterize it as Western or European.[98] The European tradition of inequality just happened to be its first target.[99]

If one accepts the basic premise of human equality, there is another ground upon which a critic of the human rights project might argue that it has been tainted by a Western, or Eurocentric, bias. It is historically true that many of the proponents of human equality believed that the concept did not extend to the whole of humanity but merely to that subset of the species that shared in the tradition known as Western Civilization. Unlike the claim that Western Civilization is synonymous with equality, that equality is a Western value, this second claim is based upon the recognition that many of those who rebelled against Western traditions of inequality had no difficulty in maintaining their belief in Western superiority. As Andre Beteille has written:

> The modern West's most dramatic denial of equality — not just the practice of equality, but the principle — was not at home but in the colonies. And so, again not unexpectedly, the colonial context is kept discreetly in the background in the many facile expositions that celebrate the triumph of egalitarianism in the West.[100]

When understood in this way equality becomes a communal value rather than a universal one. Needless to say, this restriction of the scope of the claim of equality, even when that claim is correctly cast in the form of a rebellion against Western traditions, serves the interests of those who would oppose the human rights project on the ground that it is internal to the history of the West.

---

process), this does not, in itself, invalidate the extension of the principle of equality to include all human beings in the centuries that have followed.

[98]   Characterizing the human rights movement as Western also has the curious consequence of excluding some of worst human rights abuses in history from the idea of the West. Like all other such generalizations, the West names a complex tradition of often violent oppositions rather than a coherent and lasting set of shared values.

[99]   L.J. Macfarlane, *Human Rights: Realities and Possibilities* (London: MacMillan, 1990) at 249:

> If one contrasts the human rights position in Western Europe with that existing fifty years ago the improvement is striking: the former fascist dictatorships of Italy, Germany, Spain and Portugal have all become constitutional liberal-democratic states, accepting the authority of the European Court of Human Rights to interpret and implement the European Convention on Human Rights to which they all adhere.

[100]   Andre Beteille, *The Idea of Natural Inequality and Other Essays* (New Delhi: Oxford University Press, 1983) at 36.

(4)   Negative and Positive Rights

The difference between negative and positive rights is usually expressed in terms of rights that require someone, typically, but not always, government officials, to refrain from doing something and those rights that require someone, including government officials and, more importantly, taxpayers, to do something. Positive rights, especially those requiring the intervention of governments, will as a result require the allocation of public resources to the pursuit of particular social goals. Such an allocation will in many cases require the redistribution of resources through a system of taxation. Hence, positive rights, when compared with negative rights, are commonly thought to have higher social costs. When framed in this way this distinction is also misleading, something that is clearly illustrated by the following examples.

The right "to take part in the government" (U.D.H.R., Article 21(1)) is elaborated in Article 25 of the I.C.C.P.R. to include the rights "to take part in public affairs" and the right "to vote and to be elected at genuine periodic elections". Democratic political rights, such as the right to vote, presuppose for their fulfillment the existence of elections and the expenditure of the public funds necessary to run them. They also require for their realization the existence of public offices and the staff and facilities that make the functioning of those offices possible. The existence and maintenance of an elected official requires a substantial and ongoing expenditure of public funds. The significance of this lies in the fact that democratic rights are positive entitlements rather than negative rights. Furthermore, when read as positive entitlements they oblige member states to provide the appropriate institutions.

It could be argued that political rights are not typical of the so-called negative rights. At first glance the right to own property (U.D.H.R., Article 17), or the right to privacy (U.D.H.R., Article 12) do not appear to require anything more than the restraint of one's neighbours. However, those who seek the protection of their property or their privacy routinely take it for granted that public money will be allocated to maintaining the various institutions which enforce property rights and protect privacy.[101] The link between the enforcement of these rights and human rights is rarely made because of the confusion between different senses of the distinction between

---

[101]   Peter Jones, *Rights* (Basingstoke: Macmillan, 1994) at 15 characterizes "the right not to have one's property taken" as a clear example of a "negative claim-right" without linking it to the positive claim-right to getting it back, or receiving some other form of compensation. The concept of "property" is a legal concept which presupposes the existence of a legal system willing to enforce title. This is what distinguishes property from mere possession.

public and private. The distinction between private and public law, for example, shouldn't be allowed to obscure the fact that private disputes are routinely settled in public courts at public expense. As noted earlier, access to "independent and impartial tribunals" for the settlement of such disputes is guaranteed under Article 10 of the U.D.H.R.[102] In addition, Article 14 of the I.C.C.P.R. refers to "rights and obligations in a suit of law". The right of access to an independent and impartial judiciary for the adjudication of private disputes presupposes the existence of a court system, staffed with qualified judges, which is a major public expense.[103] An independent judiciary, therefore, is not just a constitutional right, it is a positive human right. Since individuals involved in a wide range of business enterprises are among the largest users of legal services in Canada, as well as around the world, the importance of making this connection cannot be overstated.

(5)   The Generations of Rights

Another common distinction is the division of human rights into three different categories, often characterized as first, second and third generation rights. This distinction is sometimes combined with the distinction between negative and positive rights in such a way that first generation rights are said

---

[102]   Such individuals also have the human right to have these disputes resolved in a non-discriminatory fashion (U.D.H.R., art. 7).

[103]   While Canadians spend far more on health care and education, the cost of the justice system (policing, courts, corrections, but not including most private lawyers' fees), is not insignificant. In 2000-01 justice spending accounted for approximately three per cent of spending by all levels of government in Canada. This was approximately the same amount of money that was spent on national defence (*Juristat* vol. 22 no. 11 (Ottawa: Statistics Canada, 2002) at 2-3). The positive cost of "negative" rights has been recognized by a number of commentators. See, for example:

Martin Friedland, *A Place Apart: Judicial Independence and Accountability in Canada* (Ottawa: Canadian Judicial Council, 1995) at 2:

Large amounts of public resources are expended on the judicial enterprise. Money that is spent on the judiciary is necessarily not spent on other worthy endeavours.

Martha Jackman, "Constitutional Rhetoric and Social Justice" in Joel Bakan & David Schneiderman, eds., *Social Justice and the Constitution: Perspectives on a Social Union for Canada* (Ottawa: Carleton University Press, 1992) at 23:

Many classical rights, such as the right to vote, the right to a fair trial and the right to freedom of expression and association, do not come into existence automatically upon their recognition; rather, they are dependent on concerted state regulation and action, not on any absence of state compulsion and control. It is therefore simplistic to suggest that recognition and respect for classical rights imposes only negligible costs on the state.

L.J. Macfarlane, *The Theory and Practice of Human Rights* (London: Maurice Temple Smith, 1985) at 10:

[P]racticability is an issue with all human rights, not just economic and social rights, since resources are always required either for their realisation or protection.

to be negative rights while second and third generation rights are characterized as positive rights.[104] First generation rights (also called "classical rights") are said to include political and civil rights, second generation rights to include social, economic and cultural rights, and third generation rights to include collective or group rights. While not without merit from a historical perspective, this approach to human rights is both misleading and confusing. It is misleading insofar as it implies that there is a hierarchy of human rights in which political and civil rights are in some sense more important, and possibly more fundamental, than other human rights, a position that was clearly rejected in Article 5 of the Vienna Declaration. It is confusing because the use of such terms as "civil rights" and "political rights" in contexts where it isn't clear that these are types of human rights, rather than rights that can exist separately from human rights, may lead to a narrowing of the public understanding of the concept of human rights. In other words, it may further the tendency to regard human rights as being of primary concern to those whose civil and political rights are not being recognized.

Political and civil rights could exist, and did exist throughout much of history, without having the characteristics of human rights. With the advent of universal human rights this is no longer the case. The category of civil and political rights may include rights that are not human rights, just as the category of human rights contains rights that are not civil and political. Nonetheless, where the categories overlap the use of such terminology as "democratic rights", "legal rights", and "equality rights" without reference to "human rights" obscures the link between rights guaranteed in the Charter, for example, and the vocabulary of human rights which is prominent in Canadian foreign policy. One consequence of this may be that Canadians are the defenders of the human rights of others while being unable to name accurately the human rights which they themselves possess.

(6)   Human Rights and Group Rights

The phrase "group rights" is ambiguous in at least two senses.[105] It may be understood to mean respect for the rights of minorities, and the human rights they share with everyone else, or it may be interpreted to mean the existence of a special category of minority rights. This ambiguity is clearly evident in the public reaction to the rights claims made by various groups in contemporary societies. For example, the reaction of some

---

[104]   Peter Jones, *Rights* (Basingstoke: MacMillan, 1994) at 15-16.
[105]   "Minority rights" must also be distinguished from the "right to self-determination", this latter right often being claimed by minorities on the basis of their experience of colonization.

members of the public to court decisions regarding discrimination against persons with disabilities, or on the basis of sexual orientation clearly illustrates this confusion. In such cases there is a common, if not widespread, perception that the individuals involved were seeking "special" treatment. Thus, while most people in Canada are able to take it for granted that they can communicate with a physician or expect not to be fired on the basis of an irrelevant personal characteristic, when members of minorities seek protection of these rights they transform into special rights in the minds of some people.

If "minority rights" are understood as rights possessed by groups, or by the members of groups, by virtue of traits they possess which set them apart from other groups, or members of groups, then these rights cannot by definition be human rights since the latter are possessed by individuals simply by virtue of their being human. There is, of course, a human right to a national, or cultural identity, but this is not a minority right. Indeed, this right belongs to members of majorities as well. Minority rights, strictly speaking, belong to the domain of constitutional or statutory rights and as such can only be defended if they do not threaten the human rights, not only of those who do not belong to the groups possessing those rights, but also the human rights of members of the groups.

The use of the word "minority" leads to further confusion when the difference between democratic minorities and demographic minorities goes unrecognized. Democratic minorities are created by the political process; demographic minorities exist independently of the political process. For example at the time of Confederation, Protestants were a demographic minority in Lower Canada, Roman Catholics a demographic minority in Upper Canada. In each case the institution of democratic government represented a potential threat to those minorities.[106] A demographic majority, operating in the name of democracy, can use the instruments of democratic government, best exemplified in elections and in parliamentary votes, to override the legitimate interests of demographic minorities on the ground that they are democratic minorities. If democracy is misunderstood to mean "majority rule" then demographic minorities appear to be anti-democratic when they oppose the policies of the majority. They may, however, be doing nothing more than attempting to protect their own human rights and

---

[106] *Reference re Bill 30, an Act to Amend the Education Act (Ontario)*, [1987] S.C.J. No. 44 at para. 27, [1987] 1 S.C.R. 1148:

> The protection of minority religious rights was a major preoccupation during the negotiations leading to Confederation because of the perceived danger of leaving the religious minorities in both Canada East and Canada West at the mercy of overwhelming majorities.

fundamental freedoms (as distinct from minority rights) against majoritarian demands which are, misleadingly, being made in the name of democracy.

(7)   Human Rights, States and Governments

Canada's commitment to the idea of human rights is evident not only in the ratification of the international covenants but also in numerous foreign policy documents and in public statements made by political leaders and government officials. It is important to understand, therefore, to what precisely it is that Canada is committed. First, Canada is committed to taking the necessary steps to ensure that all Canadians achieve the existential status guaranteed to them under the U.D.H.R.[107] In practical terms this means that Canadians are committed to establishing and maintaining the various civil, political, economic, social and cultural institutions without which the commitment to human rights would be nothing more than empty rhetoric. Furthermore, since these institutions are themselves an expression of human rights, insofar as they derive their moral legitimacy from Canada's commitment to human rights, the various branches of government, for example, are committed to furthering the project of human rights. This means that the Canadian Government is the instrument chosen by Canadians to advance the cause of human rights. As already noted, while the majority of Canadians currently enjoy the benefits of many of these institutions, including democratic elections and an independent judiciary, they are not often encouraged to think of that enjoyment as a matter of their own human rights.

Second, Canada is committed to monitoring the performance of these institutions, not only to ensure that steps are being taken toward achieving the existential status for all Canadians (by creating the necessary institutions), but also to ensure that the institutions operate in accordance with the common standard of human rights (e.g., by dealing fairly and expeditiously with individual complaints). The project is complicated still further by the widespread belief that governments are the enemies of human rights. While there is ample evidence from around the world that government officials can be among the worst abusers of human rights, and, even in Canada, the Charter has been interpreted as a necessary protection against government, this essentially liberal view of rights tells only of the "negative" half of the story of universal human rights. The need to protect individuals from the

---

[107]   Rolf Künnemann, "A Coherent Approach to Human Rights" (1995) 17 Hum. Rts. Q. 327 has argued that:

> every (human) right is actually threefold, consisting of the right itself, the existential status linked to this right, and the State obligations following from this right.

abuse of government power presupposes the presence of a government that exists for reasons other than to abuse those who are subject to government power. Universal human rights are not intended as a protection against government *per se*, they are intended as a protection against bad government where bad governments are governments whose officials abuse the human rights of their fellow citizens. Good governments, on the other hand, are governments whose officials promote the human rights of their fellow citizens and protect those citizens from human rights abuses, not only by government officials, but also by others who are subject to the laws of the state.[108] In other words, the ideal of human rights includes the idea that "peace, order, and good government" are desirable and possible.

The problem of human rights language is complicated in other ways by the role played by government. For example, it is distressingly common to hear individuals in Canadian society refer to "the government" or "the state" as if they are alien forces in their lives, something separate from themselves. While it makes sense to speak of a monarch, an aristocracy, a military dictatorship, or the party (in single party states) as an other, this type of language distorts the relationship between the individual and the government in liberal democratic states. The problem is exacerbated by corporate leaders who routinely refer to relations between business and government using what more than one commentator has recognized as the hopelessly obscure distinction between the public and the private. In addition, the media, themselves a part of the corporate sector, treat government in ways that elide the important difference between government and state.[109] Some citizens work in the business sector, including the media, while others work in

---

[108]   K. Anthony Appiah, "Universalism and Cultural Relativism: Perspectives on the Human Rights Debate" in *Human Rights at Harvard* (Cambridge, Mass.: University Committee on Human Rights Studies, 1999) at 16:

> It is no longer enough to focus our attention on the state alone as the threat to human dignity. Our historical experience shows that the greatest threat to the autonomy and dignity of individuals comes not just from the state but from other sources ...

[109]   Christopher W. Morris, *An Essay on the Modern State* (Cambridge: Cambridge University Press, 1998) at 20-21:

> In contemporary English, especially in the United States, 'state' and 'government' are often used somewhat interchangeably. One can replace one by the other in many works of contemporary American political theory and not substantially affect the meaning of the theses defended. ... On the Continent the distinction between state and government is evident. Some remnant of the distinction may be found in British English: the prime minister is head of the *government*, while the monarch is head of the *state*. But in general no great care is taken in the English-speaking worlds to distinguish state and government. As a matter of contemporary useage, this is not possible in other European languages. *'L'Etat'* and *'le gouvernment'*, *'der Staat'* and *'die Regierung'*, *'lo stato'* and *'lo governo'* are not interchangeable. ... But the largely continental concept of the state (as distinct from the government) is in some ways alien to the Anglo-American tradition. Perhaps as a consequence of this the distinction between the two is not easily made in *contemporary English*.

governments, both federal and provincial. What all of these individuals share in common is that they are citizens (or residents) of the same state, subject to the same constitutional order and, with due allowance being made for the division of powers, to the same laws. From the standpoint of this order they are all equal, a constitutional fact given explicit formulation in section 15(1) of the Charter. Within this constitutional order some citizens occupy offices within the government, offices that are legally structured to set limits upon the activities of their occupants. The government, however, is not co-extensive with the state. The governments of Canada are the instruments chosen by the people to direct the affairs of the state, a power that is limited by the constitutional order of the state. This is what is meant by self-government. Furthermore, those who govern the state are themselves subject to the laws of the state, both constitutional and statutory. This is what is meant by rule of law.

We can use language in an effort to clarify the sources of order in our lives but the misuse of that same vocabulary can also generate confusion. Thus, we can take pride in the institution of self-government, while simultaneously distorting the meaning of self-government by the ways in which we refer to the government. The tendency toward this particular form of distortion may be somewhat more acute in multi-party states, one of the defining features of contemporary liberal democratic states, because at any given time the party in power will have been chosen by only a portion of the voting population. In such states the word "government" may be used interchangeably to refer to the government of the day, which may represent views opposed to one's own, or to the legally constituted institutions within which that government will attempt to implement its policies. This means that it is possible to be opposed to the government of the day while remaining loyal to the institutions of government.

Finally, Canada's position on human rights issues around the world derives its credibility from the evidence of Canada's domestic commitment to human rights. This is not simply a matter of establishing and maintaining institutions whose practices coincide with those required by human rights standards. It is necessary that these institutions be clearly identified with the project of human rights. The most effective way of achieving such an identification is through the enactment of legislation with the clearly stated intention of implementing Canada's international commitments by transforming human rights into legal rights, *i.e.*, rights that can be claimed as human rights within the Canadian justice system. It is up to a Canadian Government to give domestic expression to those commitments made by the Canadian state in the international legal order.

(8)   Human Rights and Legal Rights

The first and, from a practical perspective, most important difference between human rights and the various types of legal rights rests upon what is known as justiciability. A right is said to be "justiciable" when it can be claimed in a court of law. While it isn't necessary for present purposes to delve too deeply into the law of justiciability it is necessary to note that human rights *per se* are not justiciable. Neither the U.D.H.R. nor the various covenants and conventions, can be used by themselves to found a human rights claim in a Canadian court.[110] While it has been argued that human rights treaties are incorporated into Canadian law by the application of principles derived from the common law (a point to be dealt with in more detail in the discussion of treaties), there are no cases in which anyone has successfully founded a claim before a Canadian court on the basis of a human rights treaty alone.

For a right to be recognized by a court it must belong to one of the established categories of legal rights in Canada, namely, constitutional rights, statutory rights, or common law rights.[111] If a right is recognized by a court then it may be possible to persuade the court on the basis of a demonstrated infringement of the right to provide an appropriate remedy. Indeed, as noted earlier, there is a human right to such a remedy. For a human right to become a legal right it must be made part of a domestic legal order. It is in this legal form that the right becomes justiciable.

The differences among the various types of legal rights are also important. While it is true that no legal order can withstand a determined assault by those who are intent upon denying their fellow citizens' constitutionally entrenched rights, when the legal side is coupled with a truly independent judiciary, it provides a greater degree of protection than do rights protected by a statute. Statutes are subject to amendment or repeal by legislative majorities and the rights they protect are only as secure as the commitment of the government of the day to their protection. Similarly, since legislation takes precedence over the common law, any common law right can be removed by appropriately worded legislation. Any government that believes it is acting with the support of a majority may be tempted to restrict the rights of minorities or, in more extreme cases, the rights of all.

---

[110]   Lorne Sossin, Boundaries of Judicial Review: The Law of Justiciability in Canada (Toronto: Carswell, 1999) at 194:

> The enforcement of international treaties or agreements generally will not be justiciable in domestic courts unless these instruments have been incorporated into domestic law.

[111]   These would include the rights set out in the *Civil Code of Quebec* (S.Q., 1991, c. 64) which are statutory rights.

It is one of the paradoxes of human rights that rights which are declared to be universal and inalienable, require as the instrument of their actualization, constitutional and statutory rights, which are by their very nature neither universal nor inalienable. Nonetheless, it is true that, in practice, human rights have little substantive content in the absence of their finding expression as constitutional or statutory rights. However, by characterizing a legal right as a human right, it may be possible to more fully secure the legal rights by making it more difficult for legislators to remove them. For example, the equality rights set out in section 15(1) of the Charter or the right to non-discrimination established by anti-discrimination legislation may appear less secure if the fact that these are also human rights is not made explicit. While it would be naive to suggest that the mere presence of the words "human rights" is sufficient to ensure the protection of such rights, the use of these words locates these rights within the broader context of international human rights guarantees and brings into sharper focus the common interest shared by Canadians and the rest of the world's peoples in furthering the recognition and protection of such rights.

IX. THE DOMESTIC LEGAL STATUS OF HUMAN RIGHTS

The international human rights system is intended to serve as a standard against which the achievements of individual states can be measured. The system actually plays a dual role, first as a basic set of guarantees, and second as the standard by which the progress of individual states toward meeting those guarantees can be measured. This difference is important. A state's commitment to the values set out in the *International Bill of Human Rights* can be measured against those same values. One measure of this commitment is the extent to which human rights guarantees are implemented and protected within the domestic legal system of a given state. This is a matter not only of the wording of laws, but also of the presence of functioning institutions and agencies with the authority to ensure compliance with the guarantees.[112] It is well known that constitutional and statutory language alone will not suffice to protect the human rights of citizens. That said, legal enactments at the constitutional and statutory level are the necessary first steps toward implementing and protecting human rights guarantees. Furthermore, it is extremely important that such steps be taken in the name of human rights. It is at this point that the differences between

---

[112] *Principles Relating to the Status of National Institutions* (*The Paris Principles*), adopted by General Assembly Resolution 48/134 of 20 December 1993.

Canada's international human rights commitments and our domestic human rights commitments become most evident.

The legal status of the documents that make up the *International Bill of Human Rights* is complex. Like any such documents they only have legal significance for individuals if they can be used in a forum with the authority to recognize them as having the force of law. This would link the guarantees they provide to the legal institutions necessary to ensure their domestic fulfillment. While there are ways that these agreements may be used in Canadian courts the only bodies in Canada with the authority to give these rights and freedoms the full force of law are the federal, provincial and territorial legislatures. Understanding the reasons for this requires a brief examination of the difference between signing international agreements and implementing them. It will be helpful to begin by considering the difference between the U.D.H.R. and the international covenants.

The U.D.H.R. is not a treaty. Originally proclaimed as a moral document it was not intended to have the force of law. However, by the close of the 20th century some authorities on international law were arguing that the U.D.H.R. had achieved the status of what is known as "customary international law".[113] Customary international law, which arises as a result of judicial recognition of the actual practices of states, is binding on all states whether they have agreed to be bound by the law or not.[114] Unlike customary international law, treaties are only binding on parties that have actually signed and ratified them. The two international covenants, like most major human rights instruments, are treaties. There are two broadly defined models of the means by which treaty obligations may become part of domestic law, commonly referred to as "monist" and "dualist". Under a monist model the signing of the treaty is sufficient to incorporate the obligations into the domestic law of the signatory state. Treaties are, in effect, self-executing. The dualist model, as the name implies, requires a second step, namely, domestic legislation implementing the terms of the treaty. In Canada the relationship between treaties and domestic laws is dualist.[115] In the Core

---

[113] For example, in the entry for the U.D.H.R. in H. Victor Condé, *A Handbook of International Human Rights Terminology* (Lincoln: University of Nebraska Press, 1999) at 154-55 maintains "that it has now become binding ... as a matter of customary international law and is therefore binding upon all states". Other commentators, such as Oscar Schachter, have disagreed. Schachter is excerpted in Henry J. Steiner & Philip Alston, *International Human Rights in Context: Law, Politics, Morals*, 2d ed. (Oxford: Oxford University Press, 2000) at 227-31.

[114] As will be seen later, even if the U.D.H.R. has achieved this status it isn't clear precisely what this would mean within the Canadian legal system.

[115] For a discussion of monist and dualist theories of the relationship between international law and domestic law see Gibran van Ert, *Using International Law in Canadian Courts* (The Hague: Kluwer International, 2002) at 49-52. Van Ert argues that Canada is neither monist nor dualist but rather a hybrid of the two.

Document submitted to the Secretary General of the United Nations in 1998 the Government of Canada noted that:

> International conventions that Canada has ratified do not automatically become part of the law of Canada. Rather, treaties that affect the rights and obligations of individuals are implemented by domestic law. To some extent, human rights treaties are implemented by constitutional law, including the Canadian Charter of Rights and Freedoms, which applies to all governments in Canada. To a considerable extent, they are implemented by legislative and administrative measures.[116]

In the immediately following paragraph this process of implementation is qualified significantly by the comment that:

> [it] is not the practice in any jurisdiction in Canada for one single piece of legislation to be enacted incorporating a particular international human rights convention into domestic law. ... Rather, many laws and policies, adopted by federal, provincial and territorial governments, assist in the implementation of Canada's international human rights obligations.[117]

Since none of these laws explicitly implement any of the major human rights agreements it is misleading, to say the least, that they have been implemented in the legal sense of this term. It will be helpful to consider briefly a treaty that has been implemented to understand the significance of this.

The authority to enter into international agreements, the Treaty Power, rests with the executive branch of the Federal Government. When Canada signs a treaty, such as the *North American Free Trade Agreement* ("NAFTA"), the signature on the document represents a commitment at international law on the part of Canada to the other parties to the agreement. In the case of NAFTA, Canada's commitment is to the United States and Mexico. While it is common, and formally correct, to speak of states as signatories to international agreements, in practice governments sign treaties in the name of the states they govern. These commitments are made by the governments of the day, but they are binding upon the states. The signing of a treaty is an act of the executive branch of the federal government in its capacity as the representative of the Canadian state. It is this act of signing that binds Canada to the terms of the treaty. The difference between governments and states noted above is of the utmost importance in the context of international law. Obligations under international treaties are binding upon successive governments unless such governments withdraw from them.

---

[116] Core Document Forming Part of the Reports of State Parties: Canada, UN Doc HRI/CORE/1/Add.91, (12 January, 1998) at para. 137. Online: <http://www.unhchr.ch/tbs/doc.nsf/0/03fb40eed8e59cc2802565fc00544e3c?opendocument>.

[117] *Ibid.*, at para. 138.

While there are many different types of treaties, human rights treaties are known as multilateral agreements, *i.e.*, agreements between more than two states. Human rights treaties may be universal, *i.e.*, open to being signed by all of the world's states, or regional, in which case they are open to being signed only by states within a given region. The process by which treaties come into force is complex. Some treaties come into force simply by being signed by the parties that are bound by them. Others are opened for signature and enter into force when they have been signed by the number of states determined in advance as sufficient to bring them into force. The two international covenants were opened for signature in 1966, and entered into force in 1976 when the required number of states had signed them. Unlike most multilateral treaties, human rights treaties such as the international covenants are open for signature by all countries in the world. Canada ratified the covenants in 1976 and they came into force for Canada in August of that year. This does not, however, have the effect of implementing the treaty. Implementation requires the enactment of specific legislation that explicitly states the parliamentary intention of implementing the treaty. For example, the *North American Free Trade Agreement Implementation Act*,[118] as its title clearly indicates, implements Canada's obligations under NAFTA. With the exception of certain humanitarian conventions, none of the major international human rights treaties have been explicitly implemented by domestic legislation.[119]

Once a treaty is signed, ratified and implemented it becomes part of the domestic law of Canada. This means that the obligations undertaken at the international level can be invoked by Canadians in courts or before administrative tribunals in their pursuit of the various rights provided by the treaty. It is the implementing legislation and not the treaty itself that enables this to happen. Unimplemented treaties cannot be directly invoked by parties to gain standing before any Canadian court or administrative agency. No Canadian can appear before a court or an administrative tribunal solely on the ground that a right or freedom guaranteed under the *International Bill of Human Rights* has been infringed. No Canadian court or administrative

---

[118]   *North American Free Trade Agreement Implementation Act*, S.C. 1993, c. 44.

[119]   Other examples of statutes that implement international treaties include: *Anti-Personnel Mines Convention Implementation Act*, S.C. 1997, c. 33; *Chemical Weapons Convention Implementation Act*, S.C. 1995, c. 25; *Crimes Against Humanity and War Crimes Act*, S.C. 2000, c. 24 (Note: Implements the *Rome Statute Creating the International Criminal Court*); *Geneva Conventions Act*, R.S.C. 1985, c. G-3; *Bretton Woods and Related Agreements Act*, R.S.C. 1985, c. B-7; *Canadian International Trade Tribunal Act*, R.S.C. 1985, c. 47 (4th Supp.); *Special Import Measures Act*, R.S.C. 1985, c. S-15; *United Nations Foreign Arbitral Awards Convention Act*, R.S. 1985, c. 16 (2nd Supp.) (Note: Section 5 states that the Convention prevails over domestic law; s. 6 creates jurisdiction in domestic courts); *World Trade Organization Agreement Implementation Act*, S.C. 1994, c. 47; *Immigration and Refugee Protection Act*, S.C. 2001, c. 27.

tribunal is empowered to grant a remedy for any such infringement. The transition from international obligation to domestic entitlement, a transition that is routinely made in the case of economic treaties, has not been made.

The distinction between the state and the government discussed earlier is particularly significant in a state with a multi-party system because the signing of a treaty may be an expression of an ideological position on a divisive issue. For example, the debate over free trade that was central to the 1988 Federal election campaign was triggered largely by the signing of the *Canada-United States Free Trade Agreement* by the governing party of the day.[120] Since simply signing an agreement is insufficient to create binding legal obligations, the *Canada-United States Free Trade Agreement*, like its successor NAFTA, required implementing legislation.[121] It was the failure of the government to enact this legislation that triggered the election. The executive branch of the Federal Government, acting in its capacity as the representative of the state of Canada for the purposes of international relations, entered into an agreement with the United States concerning free trade. This agreement required the Government of Canada to enact legislation that would implement the agreement. To this end the executive branch of the government, acting in its capacity of providing the necessary policy skills for the Cabinet, drafted the legislation that would effectively implement the agreement. This legislation, the *Canada-United States Free Trade Agreement Implementation Act*, was passed by Parliament, where the government had a majority, but was blocked by the Senate whose approval was a necessary step in the legislative process. It wasn't until after the election, therefore, that this step could be completed. Having won an election largely fought on the issue of free trade, the government was able to enact the necessary legislation upon its return to power. Once the legislation had been proclaimed the executive, acting in its capacity as the implementer and administrator of government policies, was empowered to take the necessary steps to ensure that Canada acted in compliance with the terms of NAFTA. The process of treaty making and implementation can be seen quite clearly in this example. More recently, similar debates occurred regarding

---

[120] I have chosen international treaties regarding trade because of the close link that was originally seen by the founders of the United Nations between international trade and human rights. For example, as envisioned by Roosevelt and Churchill the post war world order "was to rest on four pillars, trade and finance on the one hand, and peace and human rights, on the other" (Christine Breining-Kaufman, "The Legal Matrix of Human Rights and Trade Law: State Obligations versus Private Rights and Obligations" in Thomas Cottier, Joost Pauwely & Elisabeth Bürgi, eds., *Human Rights and International Trade* (Oxford: Oxford University Press, 2005) at 95 at 96).

[121] *Canada-United States Free Trade Agreement Implementation Act*, S.C. 1988, c. 65.

the signing of the Kyoto Accord.[122] However, unlike the trade agreements the Kyoto Accord has not been implemented.

As the example of the *Canada-United States Free Trade Agreement* clearly shows, it does not follow from the fact that the executive has signed a treaty that the legislature will enact legislation implementing the treaty. The political will necessary to bring about the signing of a treaty will not always carry over into the will to implement it. Implementation creates the strongest possible domestic legal consequences. In implementing a treaty, the legislature will clearly indicate that the intent of the legislation is to implement the treaty, either by incorporating its terms into Canadian law or by enacting legislation that is intended to meet obligations incurred by signing the treaty. As already noted, no Canadian legislation explicitly implements any of the major international human rights agreements, either by incorporating them directly into Canadian law or by identifying them as the source of legislation. For example, neither the *Canadian Bill of Rights* nor the *Canadian Charter of Rights and Freedoms* make any reference to international human rights treaties.

One difficulty with implementing many international agreements follows from the fact that Canada is a federal state. Article 28 of the I.C.E.S.C.R. and Article 50 of the I.C.C.P.R. guarantee that "the provisions of (the covenants) shall extend to all parts of federal states without any limitations or exceptions". This means that federal states cannot use federalism as an excuse under international law for not meeting their treaty obligations. That said, the full implementation of Canada's international human rights commitments would require legislation enacted by the federal, provincial, and territorial governments. This is one of the reasons why Canada's obligations under such humanitarian agreements as the *Geneva Conventions for the Protection of War Victims* ("Geneva Conventions")[123] have been easier to implement. Although there are significant implications for the provinces and territories, the conduct of war is a matter of federal jurisdiction. The same cannot be said of human rights, many of which are clearly matters of provincial jurisdiction.

When Canada acquired the authority to enter into international agreements on its own behalf, the courts quickly held that while the treaty signing power rested with the Federal Government, it could not use the power to sign treaties as a way of overriding the division of powers in the

[122]   The Kyoto Accord was made under the *United Nations Framework Convention on Climate Change* ("U.N.F.C.C.C."). Adopted by the Third Conference of Parties ("COP3") in Kyoto, Japan on 11 December 1997, entered into force on 16 February 2005.
[123]   Approved by the *Geneva Conventions Act*, R.S. 1985, C. G-3.

Canadian constitution.[124] Thus, while the treaty power clearly belonged to the executive branch of the Federal Government, the power to enact the legislation necessary to implement the treaty obligations belonged to that legislature with the constitutional authority to legislate. Legislative authority is divided under the constitution so that only that legislature with authority over the subject matter of a treaty has the authority to implement the treaty. To return to the example of NAFTA, provincial legislation as well as federal legislation was necessary for the agreement to take effect because the agreement affected matters of provincial as well as federal jurisdiction.[125]

In addition to the problems created by the division of powers in the Canadian constitution, treaties also raise issues involving the separation of powers. Understanding the domestic legal implications of human rights treaties requires, therefore, a brief consideration of the roles of the different branches of government. Governments are commonly said to perform three different functions: legislative, adjudicative and executive. In a system of government with a true separation of powers each of these functions would be performed by a distinct branch of the government. While it is true that elected politicians, judges, and the public service carry out significantly different functions within the Canadian Government, these branches of government, as has often been pointed out, are not fully separate. Distinctions drawn between the institutions of Parliament, the courts, and the public service do not reflect clearly drawn boundaries between the functions performed by each of these branches. In a decision that explicitly dealt with the different roles played by the branches of government in protecting the rights of Canadians, a majority of the Supreme Court commented:

> While our Constitution does not expressly provide for the separation of powers ... the functional separation among the executive, legislative and judicial branches of governance has frequently been noted.[126]

---

[124]   *Reference re: Weekly Rest in Industrial Undertakings Act*, [1937] 1 D.L.R. 673 at para. 12:
> For the purposes of ss. 91 and 92, i.e., the distribution of legislative powers between the Dominion and the Provinces, there is no such thing as treaty legislation as such. The distribution is based on classes of subjects: and as a treaty deals with a particular class of subjects so will the legislative power of performing it be ascertained.

[125]   For example, the *Commercial Arbitration Act*, R.S. 1985, c. 17 (2nd Supp.) and its provincial counterparts such as the *International Commercial Arbitration Act*, R.S.O. 1990. c. I.9 implement the "Model Law on International Commercial Arbitration adopted by the United Nations Commission on International Trade Law on June 21, 1985". While these statutes do not "implement" commercial treaties such as NAFTA they create a domestic legal framework for dealing with the awards made in international commercial arbitration.

[126]   *Doucet-Boudreau v. Nova Scotia (Minister of Education)* [2003] S.C.J. No. 63, [2003] 3 S.C.R. 3 at para. 33.

In support of this claim the court's unanimous judgment in *Fraser v. Canada (Public Service Staff Relations Board)* (hereinafter "*Fraser*") was cited. In *Fraser*, the court noted:

> There is in Canada a separation of powers among the three branches of government — the legislature, the executive and the judiciary. In broad terms, the role of the judiciary is, of course, to interpret and apply the law; the role of the legislature is to decide upon and enunciate policy; the role of the executive is to administer and implement that policy.[127]

Each of these functions is relevant to understanding the implications of international treaties for Canada's domestic legal order. The relationships among those who perform them are directly relevant to the process of treaty making.

Canada is governed in accordance with a modified Westminster model of parliamentary democracy. The defining feature of the Westminster model is ministerial responsibility. This means that the heads of the various government departments, the cabinet ministers, are directly accountable to the legislature. The ministers who make up the Cabinet are elected representatives who simultaneously sit in Parliament and serve as the heads of the various departments that make up the public service. The legislative and the executive branches of the government meet in the Cabinet. In practice, therefore, the legislative and executive functions intersect in the role of the minister who must bring legislation originating in his or her department before the Parliament for approval. As an elected representative, the minister stands for the policy platform of the governing party, a platform the minister is now in a position to implement by directing the executive. It is this power to direct the executive branch of government that is fought over by political parties in the course of an election.

A great deal has been written about the relative powers of the legislature and the judiciary but the only practical power, the power to do things, belongs to the executive. In other words, the power to act is more important than the power to direct, because the exercise of the latter power always depends upon the willingness of those who possess the former to follow directions. On their own, legislators and judges are incapable of ensuring the implementation of their laws and decisions. They depend upon an obedient and compliant executive branch to carry out their policies or to enforce their judgements. One of the roles played by a constitution is to place boundaries around the directions that a majority in the legislature can give to the executive. It falls to the judiciary to police these boundaries. It is this function of the judiciary, rather than their role as interpreters and

---

[127] *Fraser v. Canada (Public Service Staff Relations Board)* [1985] S.C.J. No. 71, [1985] 2 S.C.R. 455 at para. 39.

appliers of the law, that requires a true separation of powers. Thus, under the Canadian Constitution there is a greater degree of separation between the judiciary and the legislature or the executive, than there is between the legislature and the executive.

It is important when considering the separation of powers in the Canadian context to distinguish between judicial independence and the separation of the judiciary from the other two branches of government. While judicial independence is protected under the Canadian Constitution, independent judges sit in courts that are administered by the executive branch of government and funded by acts of Parliament. It is no doubt true that individual judges sitting on individual cases are required to exercise their judgment impartially, but their control over the matters that come before them, as well as of the laws to be applied in the adjudication of those matters, is severely constrained. The inherent jurisdiction of the courts over matters of procedure and substantive law is subject to being altered or removed by Parliament. According to the most recent decisions from the Supreme Court the only function of the courts that may be constitutionally protected is judicial review.[128] It is this power, rather than the power of adjudication, that lies at the heart of the separation, as distinct from the independence, of the judiciary from the other two branches of government. There are two forms of judicial review, both of which have been, and will continue to be, significant for the role of international agreements in domestic courts.

Judicial review allows the courts to strike down legislation on the ground that it is unconstitutional, and to set aside administrative decisions on both procedural and substantive grounds. From Confederation, the judiciary have had the jurisdiction to hear challenges to legislation on the ground that a statute was enacted by a legislature, federal or provincial, lacking the appropriate constitutional authority. This well established power of the courts to strike down legislation on constitutional grounds was explicitly recognized in the *Constitution Act, 1982*, where section 52 states that "the Constitution of Canada is the supreme law of Canada, and any law that is inconsistent with the provisions of the Constitution is, to the extent of the inconsistency, of no force or effect".[129] While section 52 makes no explicit reference to the courts or the judiciary, it is a well established principle of constitutional ordering that in a state with a written constitution it is the role of the courts to determine the constitutionality of legislation. With the inclusion of the Charter in the Constitution it became possible to challenge

---

[128]   *Paul v. British Columbia (Forest Appeals Commission)*, [2003] S.C.J. No. 34, [2003] 2 S.C.R. 585 at para. 22.
[129]   *Constitution Act, 1982*, Schedule B to the *Canada Act, 1982*, (U.K.) 1982, c. 11.

the exercise of the legislative function on the ground that legislation infringes upon protected rights and freedoms.[130]

The essential difference between these two types of constitutional challenges lies in the remedy. Successful challenges on the grounds of division of powers lead to the declaration that a law could not have been enacted by the particular government, federal or provincial, that enacted it. It does not follow from this that the other order of government is prohibited from enacting such legislation. Successful challenges on Charter grounds, on the other hand, lead to the declaration that no order of government could enact such a law. A challenge based upon the division of powers is a challenge against a particular order of government while one based on the Charter is a challenge against government in general. In one example from the area of (human) rights protection in *Union Colliery v. Bryden* (hereinafter *"Union Colliery"*), a late 19th century case decided by the Judicial Committee of the Privy Council, it was held that the province of British Columbia lacked the jurisdiction to deprive Chinese males of their right to work in coal mines, not because such legislation was discriminatory, but because it violated the division of powers.[131] The Judicial Committee did not rule that the federal government lacked the jurisdiction to enact such legislation. Furthermore, in cases where the provincial government enacted discriminatory legislation within its jurisdiction, these laws were upheld by the courts.[132] In contrast to the decision in *Union Colliery*, and other early cases involving discriminatory legislation, the Supreme Court's decisions under section 15(1) of the Charter apply to the federal, provincial and territorial legislatures.

---

[130] Although its legal status was, and remains controversial, in a number of cases decided prior to 1982, the courts found what came to be known as an "implied bill of rights" in the Canadian constitution. See *Reference re Alberta Statutes* [1938] S.C.R. 100, [1938] 2 D.L.R. 81 (S.C.C.); *Saumur v. City of Quebec* [1953] 2 S.C.R. 299, [1953] 4 D.L.R. 641 (S.C.C.); *Switzman v. Elbling* [1957] S.C.J. No. 13, [1957] S.C.R. 285 (S.C.C.).

[131] *Union Colliery Co. of British Columbia v. Bryden* [1899] A.C. 580 at para. 13 (P.C.):

Their Lordships see no reason to doubt that, by virtue of s. 91, sub-s. 25, the legislature of the Dominion is invested with exclusive authority in all matters which directly concern the rights, privileges, and disabilities of the class of Chinamen who are resident in the provinces of Canada. They are also of opinion that the whole pith and substance of the enactments of s. 4 of the Coal Mines Regulation Act, in so far as objected to by the appellant company, consists in establishing a statutory prohibition which affects aliens or naturalized subjects, and therefore trench upon the exclusive authority of the Parliament of Canada.

[132] *Reference re: British Columbia Provincial Elections Act 1897*, [1903] A.C. 151 (P.C.); *R. v. Quong Wing* (1914), 49 S.C.R. 440 (S.C.C.). For a discussion of these and other pre-Charter cases involving racial discrimination see James W. St. G. Walker, *"Race," Rights and the Law in the Supreme Court of Canada* (Toronto: The Osgoode Society for Canadian Legal History and Wilfred Laurier University Press, 1997).

In addition to challenges to legislation, that is to the constitutionality of grants of statutory authority, it is also possible to bring challenges to the exercise of that authority, executive decision making, on procedural and substantive grounds. Administrative decision makers exercising statutory authority may find their decisions being challenged in the courts on the ground that they have failed to meet the duty of fairness required by their decision (procedural challenges), or that they have made an error in their interpretation or application of the law (substantive challenges). This supervisory function of the courts places the judiciary in the position of overseeing the performance of the executive branch of the government. The guiding principle adopted by the courts in performing this supervisory role is to ensure that the executive acts in compliance with the intention of the legislature, as long as the legislation falls within the boundaries of the constitution.[133] While it is not necessary to go into detail regarding the ways in which the courts have performed these functions, nor to enter into the various debates regarding the appropriate role of the courts in a democracy, it is important to recognize that each branch of government has its own role to play in meeting Canada's human rights obligations.

In the absence of the constitutional or statutory incorporation of Canada's international human rights commitments into domestic law there are, in effect, only two ways in which a court might be persuaded to make use of these agreements, namely, as materials that might help in the tasks of constitutional and statutory interpretation, and as a basis for developing the common law. Each of these uses depends upon the powers of Canadian courts set out above; each is subject to serious limitations in its application. Given the court's understandable reluctance even to appear to be judicially implementing international treaties there are, in fact, severe restrictions upon the uses that may be made of such agreements by a court.

(1)   Interpreting the Charter of Rights and Freedoms

While the two covenants came into effect in August 1976, it was 10 years before any reference was made to them by the Supreme Court. Since then the various documents that make up the *International Bill of Human Rights* have been cited by members of the Supreme Court on numerous occasions, usually in the context of interpreting the Charter. There are

---

[133]   *Spar Areospace Ltd. v. American Mobile Satellite Corporation*, [2002] S.C.J. No. 51, [2002] 4 S.C.R. 205 at para. 44:

As this Court's jurisprudence establishes, if the Court is not faced with a direct constitutional question, it generally limits the scope of its inquiry to the interpretation of a statutory provision in accordance with the sovereign intent of the legislature.

numerous sections of the Charter whose language is identical with, or sufficiently similar to, the wording found in the *International Bill of Human Rights* to permit a court's attention to be drawn toward these documents in the pursuit of an understanding of the Charter. Although originally written in a dissenting judgment, the following passage by Brian Dickson C.J. has been cited often enough to permit its being regarded as a statement of the Supreme Court's approach to the relation between international human rights agreements and the Charter:

> ... Canada is a party to a number of international human rights Conventions which contain provisions similar or identical to those in the Charter. Canada has thus obliged itself internationally to ensure within its borders the protection of certain fundamental rights and freedoms which are also contained in the Charter. The general principles of constitutional interpretation require that these international obligations be a relevant and persuasive factor in Charter interpretation. As this Court stated in *R. v. Big M Drug Mart Ltd.*, [1985] 1 S.C.R. 295, at p. 344, interpretation of the Charter must be "aimed at fulfilling the purpose of the guarantee and securing for individuals the full benefit of the Charter's protection". The content of Canada's international human rights obligations is, in my view, an important indicia of the meaning of "the full benefit of the Charter's protection". I believe that the Charter should generally be presumed to provide protection at least as great as that afforded by similar provisions in international human rights documents which Canada has ratified.

> In short, though I do not believe the judiciary is bound by the norms of international law in interpreting the Charter, these norms provide a relevant and persuasive source for interpretation of the provisions of the Charter, especially when they arise out of Canada's international obligations under human rights conventions.[134]

Two years later the above passage was quoted in a majority judgment and the principle was expanded to apply to the interpretation of section 1.

> Given the dual function of s. 1 identified in Oakes, Canada's international human rights obligations should inform not only the interpretation of the content of the rights guaranteed by the Charter but also the interpretation of what can constitute pressing and substantial s. 1 objectives which may justify restrictions upon those rights. Furthermore, for purposes of this stage of the proportionality inquiry, the fact that a value has the status of an international human right, either in customary international law or under a treaty to which Canada is a State Party, should generally be indicative of a high degree of importance attached to that objective.[135]

---

[134] *Reference Re Public Service Employee Relations Act (Alberta)*, [1987] S.C.J. No. 10, [1987] 1 S.C.R. 313 at paras. 59-60, Dickson C.J. dissenting (hereinafter "*Public Service*").
[135] *Slaight Communications v. Davidson*, [1989] S.C.J. No. 45, [1989] 1 S.C.R. 1038 at para. 23, Dickson C.J. for the majority (hereinafter "*Slaight*"). Both *Public Service* and *Slaight* were cited more recently in *United States of America v. Burns*, [2001] S.C.J. No. 8, [2001] 1 S.C.R. 283.

Clearly, this approach requires a court to make itself aware of the provisions in the *International Bill of Human Rights* when interpreting the Charter.

(2) Judicial Interpretation of Statutory Language

There is a longstanding principle of British constitutionalism that the executive branch of the government cannot usurp the law making power of the legislature. Insofar as Canada may be said to have "a constitution similar in principle to that of the United Kingdom" the idea that only Parliament, and the provincial and territorial legislatures, can enact laws is central to the Canadian constitutional order. That said the lawmaking process is much more complex than this relatively simple characterization implies. While it is true that legislation cannot simply be proclaimed by the party in power, on any given day the bills brought before Parliament, and the various provincial and territorial legislatures, are drafted by the executive branch and are subject to being declared unconstitutional by the judiciary. Furthermore, the meaning to be given to statutory language will eventually be determined by the executive branch in the course of administering the laws, under the supervision of the courts which have the final say on the meaning of that language. However, in their interpretations the courts will endeavour to give effect to the intentions of the legislature, one of which will clearly be the intention to implement a treaty. In the absence of explicit implementing language, the courts will not assume the role of treaty-implementation although they will, under certain circumstances to be considered below, take the existence of unimplemented international agreements into account.

While it is a well established principle of the common law of statutory interpretation that the legislature will be presumed not to have enacted legislation that is at odds with Canada's international commitments, this presumption only applies in cases where it is necessary to resolve an ambiguity. As Pigeon J. remarked in *Daniels v. White*:

> I wish to add that, in my view, this is a case for the application of the rule of construction that Parliament is not presumed to legislate in breach of a treaty or in any manner inconsistent with the comity of nations and the established rules of international law. It is a rule that is not often applied, because if a statute is unambiguous, its provisions must be followed even if they are contrary to international law. ...[136]

In other words, the courts will not enforce Canada's international obligations, even in the case of treaties that have been implemented through

---

[136] *Daniels v. White*, [1968] S.C.J. No. 33, [1968] S.C.R. 517 at 541, Pigeon J.; cited in *Schreiber v. Canada*, [2002] S.C.J. No. 63, [2002] 3 S.C.R. 269, LeBel J. for the court at para. 50.

legislation, if the legislature clearly enacts legislation in violation of those obligations.[137]

(3) Developing the Common Law

There is another possible way in which international human rights agreements might be used by the courts, namely, through influencing the development of the common law. International law includes not only bilateral and multilateral treaties, but also what is known as customary international law. This is a body of law that is created through judicial recognition of state practices. In addition, international law includes a number of fundamental rules that are known as peremptory norms, or *jus cogens*.[138] It has been held that customary international law, is part of the common law.[139] Since the U.D.H.R. is now recognized as having the status of customary international law, it is possible that a common law court might hold that the various Articles of this document have been incorporated into the common law. Needless to say, nothing like this has been done to date. While some parts of the U.D.H.R. such as the prohibitions against slavery and torture, can be said to have achieved the status of *jus cogens*, or peremptory norms, under international law many of the signatories of the U.D.H.R. would likely vigorously protest against the extension of this category to include social and economic rights.[140] Indeed, social and economic rights are commonly regarded as being qualified by the availability of resources within a state, a qualification that does not, and

---

[137] Mark Freeman & Gibran van Ert, *International Human Rights Law* (Toronto: Irwin Law, 2004) at 173:

> Since nothing in the written constitution expressly forbids legislatures from enacting laws which violate international law, Parliament and the Legislatures may do so. The power of our legislatures to violate international law has been frequently affirmed.

[138] A norm that has achieved this status cannot be violated by any state. For example, a treaty between two states that derogated from such norms would not be recognized as valid under international law.

[139] For recent discussions of the status of customary international law in Canadian law see: Gibran Van Ert, *Using International Law in Canadian Courts* (The Hague: Kluwer, 2002) at 19-22, 137-70; Mark Freeman and Gibran Van Ert, *International Human Rights Law* (Toronto: Irwin Law, 2004) at 159-64; Hugh Kindred and Phillip M. Saunders, *et. al.*, *International Law Chiefly as Interpreted and Applied in Canada*, 7th ed., (Toronto: Emond Montgomery, 2006) at 186-94; *Crossing Borders: Law in a Globalized World* (Ottawa: Law Commission of Canada, 2006) at 29-30.

[140] There was general agreement at the time it was drafted and proclaimed that the U.D.H.R. was not intended to have legal status. As Eleanor Roosevelt noted:

> It is not a treaty; it is not an international agreement. It is not and does not purport to be a statement of law or of legal obligation.

Quoted in H. Lauterpacht, *International Law and Human Rights* (London: Steven & Sons, 1950) at 398-99.

should not, apply in the case of rights that have achieved the status of peremptory norms. Recognizing the U.D.H.R. as part of the common law by virtue of its status at international law would create similar problems. Therefore, if the integrity of the document is to be maintained there is good reason for being cautious about any approach that would further the idea that some human rights are more worthy of protection than others. Indeed, it is precisely this approach to the human rights project that has resulted in the fragmented Canadian human rights landscape in which the original vision has been all but lost. In the next, and final section, the fate of two attempts by the courts to extend the common law by using Canada's international obligations as evidence of public policy will be briefly examined within the larger context of the evolution of human rights protection in Canada.

X.   AN UNFINISHED PROJECT

Entrenched bills of rights, like human rights legislation, are expressions of political will and not creations of the courts. It is important to remember that the legal concept of discrimination in Canada was created by democratically elected legislatures, not by the courts. Indeed, prior to the enactment of human rights legislation in Canada the courts, with one justly famous exception, had refused to recognize the existence of discrimination as a legally remediable harm. The exception, quickly overruled by an appellate court in a different case, was the judgment of MacKay J. in the 1945 Ontario case *Re Drummond Wren*.[141] Canadian courts have an inherent jurisdiction over the development of the common law, a body of law long recognized as open to the possibility of judicial adjustment in response to social, political, and economic changes. The common law does not, however, change dramatically at any point in time. Adjustments, when they occur, are incremental. Furthermore, all common law is subject to being displaced by clearly worded statutory language, so the protection provided by the common law recognition of human rights would not be any greater than that provided by statute, and would be significantly less than that provided by those sections of the Charter that are not subject to the possibility of a statutory override.

Re Drummond Wren concerned what is known as a restrictive covenant on a title deed. The purpose of such covenants is to place limitations on the holder of the title regarding the uses that may be made of the property. The covenant at issue in *Re Drummond Wren* restricted the categories of persons to whom the property could be sold. More precisely,

---

[141]   *Re Drummond Wren*, [1945] O.J. No. 546, [1945] O.R. 778 (H.C.J.).

the title to the property included a covenant prohibiting the sale of the property to "Jews or persons of objectionable nationality". Restrictive covenants of this sort were common throughout North America before the Second World War and it wasn't until 1951 that the Supreme Court of Canada ruled them unacceptable, although not on the ground that they were discriminatory.

Justice Mackay's reasoning in *Re Drummond Wren* captured the changing climate of global opinion at precisely the moment when the world was beginning to recognize the full implications of the Second World War. The United Nations had formally begun operations on October 24, only a week before he released his judgment. Canada would ratify the Charter of the United Nations nine days later thereby becoming one of the original members. In his reasons Mackay J. drew attention to various recent events, including the founding of the United Nations, to support his argument that public policy in the Province of Ontario, reflecting changes clearly occurring elsewhere, now supported the creation of a legal remedy for an act of discrimination. It was Mackay J.'s use of the common law argument from public policy that was to be rejected three years later.

Writing in a subsequent case involving a restrictive covenant, *Re Noble and Wolf*,[142] Schroeder J. of the Ontario High Court drew attention to the fact that there was no domestic legislation in Canada, federal or provincial, that gave effect to any obligations Canada might have incurred as a result of becoming a member of the United Nations. The restrictive covenant at issue in this later case was both more precise and more far reaching than that in *Re Drummond Wren*. It prohibited the "ownership, use, occupation and enjoyment" of the lands in question "by any person of the Jewish, Hebrew, Semitic, Negro or coloured race or blood" and, for greater certainty, went on to restrict access to the lands "to persons of the white or Caucasian race". In a decision released six months before the General Assembly proclaimed the U.D.H.R., Schroeder J. held that if anything was to be done about the problem of restrictive covenants it was up to the legislature to take action.

A year later, the Chief Justice of Ontario, in upholding the judgment of the lower court, drew attention to what he regarded as the limitation of law as a means of dealing with the problem of discrimination:

> Doubtless, mutual goodwill and esteem among the people of the numerous races that inhabit Canada is greatly to be desired, and the same goodwill and esteem should extend abroad, but what is so desirable is not a mere show of goodwill or a pretended esteem, such as might be assumed to comply with a law made to enforce it. To be worth anything, either at home or abroad, there is required the goodwill and esteem of a free people, who genuinely

---

[142] *Re Noble and Wolf*, [1948] O.J. No. 485, [1948] O.R. 579 (H.C.J.).

feel, and sincerely act upon, the sentiments they express. A wise appreciation of the impotence of laws in the development of such genuine sentiments, rather than mere formal observances, no doubt restrains our legislators from enacting, and should restrain our Courts from propounding, rules of law to enforce what can only be of natural growth, if it is to be of any value to anyone.[143]

Chief Justice Robertson's argument that the law is unable to correct human sentiments clearly sidesteps the real issue of the power of the law to correct injustice.[144] As the courts were later to recognize, when upholding decisions made by human rights tribunals, it is not the intent to discriminate that causes the harm, it is the wrong of discrimination that must be remedied.[145]

The closest a Canadian court has come to using the U.D.H.R. as the basis for a change in the common law since *Re Drummond Wren* was the attempt by Wilson J., while serving on the Ontario Court of Appeal, to create a tort of discrimination. The ensuing disagreement between her and Laskin C.J., who wrote the majority judgment in which she was overruled by the Supreme Court, is instructive. In *Bhadauria v. Board of Governors of Seneca College*, Wilson J. remarked that:

> While the fundamental human right we are concerned with (the right not to be discriminated against) is recognized by the (Ontario Human Rights) Code, it was not created by it.[146]

In support of this view she cited the Preamble to the Code which contained a reference to the *Universal Declaration of Human Rights*. While the Code did not claim to be implementing any of Canada's international obligations, it does appear to have been enacted in recognition of those obligations. It was this distinction that was rejected by Laskin J.

In *Seneca College v. Bhadauria* Laskin C.J. replied to Wilson J. as follows:

> I confess to some difficulty in understanding the basis of the learned justice's observation that "While the fundamental human right we are concerned with is recognized by the Code, it was not created by it" (or, I

---

[143]   *Re Noble and Wolf*, [1949] O.J. No. 466, [1949] O.R. 503 (C.A.).

[144]   The Ontario Court of Appeal was overruled by the Supreme Court without addressing the issue of discrimination (*Noble v. Alley*, [1951] S.C.R. 64 (S.C.C.)). Restrictive covenants of the type challenged in *Re Drummond Wren* and *Noble Wolf* were made illegal by the Ontario legislature in 1950. For a detailed discussion of *Noble Wolf* and its consequences, see James W. St. G. Walker, *"Race," Rights and the Law in the Supreme Court of Canada* (Toronto: The Osgoode Society and Wilfrid Laurier University Press, 1997) at 182-245.

[145]   The Canadian courts have held that proof of intention is not a necessary element in the discrimination prohibited by human rights legislation (*Ontario (Human Rights Commission) v. Simpsons Sears Ltd.*, [1985] S.C.J. No. 74, [1985] 2 S.C.R. 536 at para. 14).

[146]   *Bhadauria v. Board of Governors of Seneca College of Applied Arts and Technology*, [1979] O.J. No. 4475, 27 O.R. (2d) 142 at 150 (C.A.).

assume, by its predecessors). There is no gainsaying the right of the Legislature to establish new rights or to create new interests of which the Court may properly take notice and enforce, either under the prescriptions of the Legislature or by applying its own techniques if, on its construction of the legislation, enforcement has not been wholly embraced by the terms of the legislation.[147]

According to Laskin C.J. human rights legislation had overtaken the "common law in Ontario and established a different regime which does not exclude the courts but rather makes them part of the enforcement machinery under the Code".[148]

In the end the disagreement between Wilson J. and Laskin C.J. regarding the difference between creating rights and recognizing rights can be partially resolved by noting that Wilson J. was correct in holding that the Code recognized the human right not to be discriminated against, while Laskin C.J. was also correct to insist that the statute had created the remedy for violations of that right. Indeed, their disagreement draws attention once again to the difference discussed earlier between having human rights and enjoying the legal recognition of those rights, a recognition that requires the availability of remedies. In her judgment Wilson J. relied upon an early 18th century English judgment, *Ashby v. White*. In that case the court held:

> If the plaintiff has a right, he must of necessity have a means to vindicate and maintain it, and a remedy if he is injured in the exercise or enjoyment of it; and indeed it is a vain thing to imagine a right without a remedy; for want of right and want of remedy are reciprocal.[149]

While this reciprocal link between a right and a remedy clearly applies in the case of legal rights it does not, as noted earlier, apply to human rights. If the law, whether constitutional, statutory or common, does not recognize a right then it follows that the law will not provide a remedy for a harm based on the denial of that right. However, it doesn't follow from the fact that if one does not have a legal remedy that one does not have a human right. It is only once a human right has been transformed into a legal right that one acquires a remedy.

It was democratically elected provincial legislatures, beginning with Saskatchewan, that enacted statutes creating legal remedies for those harmed by discrimination. By the close of the 1950's most Canadian provinces had enacted legislation dealing with discrimination. Ontario's Anti-Discrimination Commission (later the Ontario Human Rights Commission),

---

[147] *Seneca College of Applied Arts and Technology v. Bhadauria*, [1981] S.C.J. No. 76, [1981] 2 S.C.R. 181 at 193-94 (hereinafter "*Bhadauria*").

[148] *Ibid.*, at 195.

[149] *Ashby v. White* (1703), 2 Ld. Raym. 938 at 953 (H.L.).

the first of its kind in Canada, was established in 1958. Put another way, the legal concept of discrimination is a creation of the legislature, an expression of political will, not the product of judicial decision making. While the courts will have a role in the development of the legal definition of "discrimination" that role will require constant reference back to the legislation.[150]

Almost four years after the Supreme Court's decision in *Bhadauria*, section 15 of the Charter came into effect. The section had been delayed for three years because the authors of the Charter rightly believed that the immediate consequences of entrenching the Charter would be most fully felt in the area of equality rights. In addition, equality and discrimination had been among the more controversial concepts during the negotiations that led to the drafting of the final version of the Charter. In its first ruling on section 15, in *The Law Society of British Columbia v. Andrews* (hereinafter "*Andrews*") the Supreme Court drew attention to the relationship between the concept of discrimination in the Charter and the prior evolution of that concept in the jurisprudence deriving from human rights legislation. Commenting upon the problem of defining "discrimination" McIntyre J. noted:

> What does discrimination mean? The question has arisen most commonly in a consideration of the Human Rights Acts and the general concept of discrimination under those enactments has been fairly well settled. There is little difficulty, drawing upon the cases in this Court, in isolating an acceptable definition.[151]

The effect of the court's judgment in *Andrews* was twofold. First, the court affirmed that the origin of the concept of discrimination was to be found in two political acts, namely, the enactment of human rights legislation and the entrenching of section 15(1) of the Charter in the Canadian Constitution. Second, by citing its own earlier judgments on appeals from the decisions of human rights tribunals, the court clearly asserted its role in the ongoing process of refining the concept.

---

[150] It is a matter of some significance that future Chief Justice Laskin is reported to have largely written the brief to the court in *Re Drummond Wren* in which the argument from public policy, accepted by Mackay J., was advanced. This underscores his remark in *Bhadauria* that while he himself did "not quarrel with the approach taken in *Re Drummond Wren*", the decision had been overruled. Laskin was also involved, this time on the losing side, in *Noble v. Wolf* before the Ontario courts. In addition, he advocated for the implementation of the U.D.H.R. and was involved in the drafting of early anti-discrimination legislation in Ontario. For an account of Laskin C.J.'s involvement in human rights activities see Philip Girard, *Bringing the Law to Life* (Toronto: University of Toronto Press, 2005) at 247-71. For accounts of the disagreement between Laskin C.J. and Wilson J. over *Bhadauria* see Girard, *ibid.* at 492-95; Ellen Anderson, *Judging Bertha Wilson: Law as Large as Life* (Toronto: University of Toronto, 2001) at 121-24.
[151] *Law Society of British Columbia v. Andrews*, [1989] S.C.J. No. 6, [1989] 1 S.C.R. 143 at para. 37.

The full complexity of the still evolving relationship between human rights legislation and section 15 of the Charter need not be explored here. Nonetheless, there are several features of this relationship that are worth mentioning. In an early section 15 case concerning mandatory retirement, *McKinney v. The University of Guelph* (hereinafter "*McKinney*"), the court ruled that while private (non-governmental) actors could not directly invoke the Charter concept of discrimination in their dealings with one other, they could use the Charter to challenge the human rights legislation that did apply to those dealings.[152] While neither of the pieces of this combination were particularly original, *McKinney* clearly established the principle that the concept of discrimination in human rights legislation would have to develop along lines that were consistent with developments in the section 15 concept. The most significant application of this principle was to occur less than a decade later in the Supreme Court's decision in *Vriend v. Alberta* (hereinafter "*Vriend*").[153]

The issue before the court in *Vriend* was the refusal of the legislature of Alberta to include sexual orientation as a prohibited ground of discrimination in its human rights legislation. Addressing the controversy over the court's role in this case, Iacobucci J. drew attention to the source of the court's authority to invalidate legislation on the ground that it violated the Charter:

> [It] should be emphasized again that our Charter's introduction and the consequential remedial role of the courts were choices of the Canadian people through their elected representatives as part of a redefinition of our democracy. Our constitutional design was refashioned to state that henceforth the legislatures and executive must perform their roles in conformity with the newly conferred constitutional rights and freedoms. That the courts were the trustees of these rights insofar as disputes arose concerning their interpretation was a necessary part of this new design.[154]

Once again the same two assertions from *Andrews* are present. Opposition to discrimination reflects the political will of the Canadian people and once that opposition has been entrenched in the constitution the final authority for giving legal definition to that opposition must rest with the courts.[155]

The year after the decision in *Vriend* the close relationship between section 15(1) and human rights legislation was reinforced in a judgment of the Supreme Court that did not involve the Charter. In the *British Columbia*

[152] *McKinney v. University of Guelph*, [1990] S.C.J. No. 122, [1990] 3 S.C.R. 229.
[153] *Vriend v. Alberta*, [1998] S.C.J. No. 29, [1998] 1 S.C.R. 493.
[154] *Ibid.*, at para. 134.
[155] While Iacobucci J. did not raise the issue in *Vriend*, under the Charter the legislature retains the authority to give expression to a change in the political will by invoking s. 33, the notwithstanding clause.

(Public Service Relations Commission) v. British Columbia Government and Service Employees' Union (B.C.G.E.U.) (hereinafter "*Méiorin*") decision the court redefined the relationship between direct and adverse effect discrimination. In her discussion of the reasons underlying her decision McLachlin J. noted that there was a "dissonance between human rights analysis and *Charter* analysis" of the concept of discrimination. After a brief characterization of this dissonance she concluded:

> I see little reason for adopting a different approach when the claim is brought under human rights legislation which, while it may have a different legal orientation, is aimed at *the same general wrong* as s. 15(1) of the *Charter*.[156] [Emphasis added.]

Justice McLachlin's conclusion clearly affirms that insofar as it is intended to remedy "the same general wrong", the concept of discrimination should have a single meaning in Canadian law. This is one of the reasons why it is unfortunate that the concept of the human right not to be discriminated against has become isolated from its context in the more broadly defined human rights project. As shown earlier, the link between this human right and all of the others is clearly evident in the major international human rights agreements to which Canada is a party. The link would also have been more apparent in the domestic legal order if the original vision of the Canadian Charter had been realised.

Speaking in the House of Commons on July 1, 1960 Prime Minister John G. Diefenbaker addressed the reasons for enacting the *Canadian Bill of Rights*:

> This measure that I introduce is the first step on the part of Canada to carry out the acceptance either of the international declaration of human rights or of the principles that actuated those who produced that noble document.[157]

While it never enjoyed the success anticipated by its proponents, the *Bill of Rights* was, as the foregoing passage clearly illustrates, intended to be the first step on a much longer journey. The second step was the *Charter of Rights and Freedoms*. The story of how the Charter came to be part of the project to patriate the Canadian Constitution has been told many times.[158]

---

[156]   *British Columbia (Public Service Relations Commission) v. British Columbia Government and Service Employees' Union (B.C.G.E.U.) (Méiorin Grievance)*, [1999] S.C.J. No. 46, [1999] 3 S.C.R. 3 at para. 48.

[157]   Prime Minister Diefenbaker preceded this remark by reading in full the Preamble to the U.D.H.R. (John Diefenbaker "Human Rights in Canada" Speech to the House of Commons (24th Parliament, 3rd Session, 1960), *Debates* vol. V, at 4815-5818 (Ottawa: Queen's Printer, 1960)).

[158]   See, for example: Robert Sheppard and Michael Valpy, *The National Deal: The Fight for a Canadian Constitution* (Toronto: Fleet Books, 1982); Roy Romanow, John Whyte & Howard

The following comments will be restricted to a brief consideration of the relation between the Charter and Canada's international human rights commitments.

In a policy paper issued in 1968 entitled, *A Canadian Charter of Human Rights*, the Government of Canada re-opened discussion of the possibility of entrenching human rights protection in the constitution.[159] The scope of this protection was considered with specific reference to the U.D.H.R. and the two international covenants which had only recently been opened for signature. Economic rights such as the rights to work, social security, an adequate standard of living and an education were acknowledged but it was recognized that the time was not right for entrenching them in the constitution:

> The guarantee of such economic rights is desirable and should be an ultimate objective for Canada. There are, however, good reasons for putting aside this issue at this stage and proceeding with the protection of political, legal, egalitarian and linguistic rights. It might take considerable time to reach agreement on the rights to be guaranteed and on the feasibility of implementation. The United Nations recognized these problems when it prepared two separate Covenants on Human Rights — one on Civil and Political Rights and one on Economic, Social and Cultural Rights, thus giving nations an opportunity to accede to them one at a time.[160]

In other words, the project of entrenching economic and social rights was to be postponed, not abandoned.

The following year, in a document entitled *The Constitution and the People of Canada*, Prime Minister Pierre Trudeau presented to participants in the Second Meeting of the Constitutional Conference a proposal to include a statement of "the four objectives of Confederation" to be included in a preamble to the Canadian Constitution.[161] While the first objective was a commitment to "a federal system of government based on democratic principles" the remaining three all concerned aspects of the project of human rights. They are worth setting out in full:

> To protect basic human rights, which shall include linguistic rights.
>
> To promote national economic, social and cultural development, and the general welfare and equality of opportunity for all Canadians in whatever region they may live, including the opportunity for gainful work, for just

---

Leeson, *Canada – Notwithstanding: the making of the Constitution, 1976-1982* (Toronto: Carswell/Methuen, 1984).

[159] Department of Justice, *A Canadian Charter of Human Rights* (Ottawa: Queen's Printer, 1968).

[160] *Ibid.*, at 27.

[161] *The Constitution and the People of Canada: Constitutional Conference 1969* (Ottawa: Government of Canada, 1969).

conditions of employment, for an adequate standard of living, for security, for education, and for rest and leisure.

To contribute to the achievement of world peace and security, social progress and better standards of life for all mankind.[162]

In the end a preamble was not included in the *Constitution Act, 1982* although there is a brief preamble to the *Charter of Rights and Freedoms*, the document that resulted from the constitutional negotiations.[163] By the time that document was included in the new constitution the word "human" had disappeared from its title.

Less than 20 years after the Charter became part of the law of Canada, the Supreme Court, in their decision on the possible secession of Quebec, identified four basic principles of the Canadian constitutional order: federalism, democracy, rule of law, and the protection of minorities.[164] Once again there is no reference to human rights. Thus, in spite of the fact that the Charter was originally intended to affirm Canada's commitment to the domestic implementation of the project of human rights, the link to the scope of that project as envisioned in the *International Bill of Human Rights*, was obscured in the final document. The link might have been made by retaining the name *Charter of Human Rights* or by including a reference to human rights in the Preamble but clearly this was not done.

Human rights language in Canada can be found in the constitution, federal and provincial statutes and in the various international agreements to which Canada is signatory. In each of these contexts human rights, either explicitly or implicitly, are characterized as "fundamental" or "quasi fundamental" and governments are charged with the task of protecting them. However, if human rights are more fundamental than constitutions, which are in turn more fundamental than anti-discrimination statutes, which are in their turn more fundamental than ordinary legislation, then references to human rights in each of these contexts should be made consistent with their shared foundation in international human rights instruments, most significantly, the *International Bill of Human Rights*. Consistency among references does not mean, that the definitions of the rights will be the same in each and every case.[165] On the contrary, the meaning of human rights is,

---

[162]   *Ibid.*, at 48.

[163]   Dale Gibson, *The Law of the Charter: General Principles* (Toronto: Carswell, 1986) at 65:
      The words of the preamble ... stand in stark contrast to the eloquent and often lengthy
      statements of purpose and principle with which national and international human rights
      documents are customarily prefaced.

[164]   *Reference re Secession of Quebec*, [1998] S.C.J. No. 61, [1998] 2 S.C.R. 217 at para. 49.

[165]   According to the Supreme Court:
      a constitution may provide an added safeguard for fundamental human rights and
      individual freedoms which might otherwise be susceptible to government interference.

and will undoubtedly remain, the subject of ongoing debate. References to human rights are consistent when the same sources of interpretation are intended in each case and when the relation among the various texts remains stable.

If the vocabulary of the U.D.H.R. is to function as a "common standard" then the Canadian interpretation of this language should develop consistently, in the sense defined above, with this vocabulary. This means that those charged with the task of furthering the project of human rights must choose between doing so in the name of traditional Canadian values or doing so in the name of human rights. The latter course, which is consistent with the U.D.H.R., requires that an effort be made to inform Canadians that the foundation of their rights and freedoms, as well as of their duties and responsibilities, has shifted from local tradition to a universal source of moral norms. While the Canadian identity may be said to include "respect for human rights" this respect presupposes the existence of the rights. Once again, human rights only exist when they are called by that name. If human rights are to be recognized as human rights, and if they are truly to be foundational, then they must be identified as such wherever rights are being discussed. Only then will there be a chance that human rights may "become the common language of humanity".

This formulation of the relationship between a constitution and human rights clearly recognizes the primacy of the latter (*Reference re Secession of Quebec*, [1998] S.C.J. No. 61, [1998] 2 S.C.R. 217 at para. 74).

A SELECTION OF HUMAN RIGHTS MATERIALS

A NOTE ON THE SELECTION OF MATERIALS

In keeping with the foregoing introduction and commentary, the following selection of human rights materials focuses upon the language of human rights rather than upon the institutions that have been established to advance and protect those rights. Once proclaimed the ideal of human rights took its place as part of the common heritage of all human beings, a status it will retain regardless of the success or failure of the various institutions with which that ideal has come to be associated. For example, while the *Universal Declaration of Human Rights*[1] ("U.D.H.R.") was proclaimed by the General Assembly of the United Nations, its value as a moral foundation for economic, social, cultural, legal, and political practices is not dependent upon the survival of that body. Indeed, human rights bodies at the national and international levels, both governmental and non-governmental, must themselves be subject to ongoing evaluation on the basis of the vision set out in the U.D.H.R. and the two international covenants.[2] These three documents are, and will remain, the starting point for the human rights project.

In selecting the remaining materials a number of considerations were taken into account. As a rule none of the selections is likely to be amended in the near future. Some of the documents are either treaties of longstanding or, in the case of the *Canadian Charter of Rights and Freedoms*,[3] constitutionally entrenched. While it is possible that the *Canadian Bill of Rights*[4] and the various selections from federal and provincial legislation might be amended at some point, it is less likely that

---

[1]   G.A. Res. 217A (111), U.N. GAOR 3d Sess., Supp. No. 13, U.N. Doc A/810 (1948) 71.

[2]   *International Covenant on Economic, Social and Cultural Rights* ("I.C.E.S.C.R."), 16 December 1966, 993 U.N.T.S. 3 (entered into force 3 January 1976, accession by Canada 19 May 1976); *International Covenant on Civil and Political Rights* ("I.C.C.P.R."), 16 December 1966, 999 U.N.T.S. 171 (entered into force 23 March 1976, accession by Canada 19 May 1999).

[3]   Part I of the *Constitution Act, 1982*, being Schedule B to the *Canada Act 1982* (U.K.), 1982, c. 11 ("Charter").

[4]   S.C. 1960, c. 44 ("Bill").

any such amendments would alter their preambles, statements of purpose and lists of basic rights.

The selections were also made with a view to representing the widest possible range of legal forms in which human rights protection may be established. While some would maintain that the U.D.H.R. has achieved legal status at international law, it is unarguably what its framers intended it to be, a proclamation of a set of moral values, a call to the people of the world to strive to establish laws that would give effect to the ideals expressed in its various articles. The international covenants and conventions are examples of multilateral treaties open for signature by all countries in the world while the *American Declaration of the Rights and Duties of Man*[5] and the convention are examples of regional agreements. The opening excerpt from the *Vienna Declaration and Programme of Action*[6] is included because it demonstrates the ongoing commitment of representatives of the community of nations, including Canada, to the ideals first set out in the U.D.H.R.

Within the domestic Canadian legal order the Charter follows logically, albeit not legally, from the international agreements. Although they form an essential part of human rights protection, federal, provincial and territorial human rights statutes (anti-discrimination legislation) have not been included in their entirety, not only because they are subject to regular amendments, but also because much of their content is concerned with the administrative machinery of anti-discrimination regimes rather than with the statement of the broader scope of the human rights project. The anti-discrimination provisions set out in the *Canadian Human Rights Act*[7] have been chosen to represent the type of protection that is currently available in "human rights legislation". Sections of several other federal statutes have been included as illustrations of Canada's commitment to the international human rights project. Excerpts from provincial and territorial human rights statutes have been included for two reasons. Although the *Canadian Human Rights Act* does not include a preamble, many provincial human rights statutes contain either preambles of statements of purpose. It is in these provisions that references to the U.D.H.R., whether explicit or implicit, are most commonly found in legislation within Canada. In addition, three provinces and one territory have enacted bills

---

[5]   O.A.S. Res. XXX, adopted by the Ninth International Conference of American States (1948), reprinted in Basic Documents pertaining to Human Rights in the Inter-American System, OEA/Ser.L.V/II.82 doc. 6 rev. 1 at 17 (1992).

[6]   United Nations World Conference on Human Rights: Vienna Declaration and Programme of Action, UN Doc. A/Conf. 157/24 (1993).

[7]   R.S., 1985, c. H-6.

of rights which extend rights protection in those jurisdictions beyond the normal boundaries of anti-discrimination legislation. The Alberta *Bill of Rights*,[8] the Quebec *Charter of Human Rights and Freedoms*[9] and the *Canadian Bill of Rights* are the only pieces of legislation in Canada that clearly state within the body of a statute that Canadians have human rights, however limited the list of those rights turns out to be.

I.   INTERNATIONAL

1.   Charter of the United Nations

June 26 1945, 59 Stat. 1031, T.S. 993, 3 Bevans 1153, entered into force Oct. 24, 1945.

Preamble

WE THE PEOPLES OF THE UNITED NATIONS DETERMINED

To save succeeding generations from the scourge of war, which twice in our lifetime has brought untold sorrow to mankind, and

To reaffirm faith in fundamental human rights, in the dignity and worth of the human person, in the equal rights of men and women and of nations large and small, and

To establish conditions under which justice and respect for the obligations arising from treaties and other sources of international law can be maintained, and

To promote social progress and better standards of life in larger freedom,

AND FOR THESE ENDS

To practice tolerance and live together in peace with one another as good neighbors, and

To unite our strength to maintain international peace and security, and

To ensure by the acceptance of principles and the institution of methods, that armed force shall not be used, save in the common interest, and

To employ international machinery for the promotion of the economic and social advancement of all peoples,

---

[8]   R.S.A. 2000, O.A.-14.
[9]   R.S.Q. c. C-12.

HAVE RESOLVED TO COMBINE OUR EFFORTS TO ACCOMPLISH THESE AIMS

Accordingly, our respective Governments, through representatives assembled in the city of San Francisco, who have exhibited their full powers found to be in good and due form, have agreed to the present Charter of the United Nations and do hereby establish an international organization to be known as the United Nations.

Chapter I
Purposes and Principles

Article 1

The Purposes of the United Nations are:

1. To maintain international peace and security, and to that end: to take effective collective measures for the prevention and removal of threats to the peace, and for the suppression of acts of aggression or other breaches of the peace, and to bring about by peaceful means, and in conformity with the principles of justice and international law, adjustment or settlement of international disputes or situations which might lead to a breach of the peace;

2. To develop friendly relations among nations based on respect for the principle of equal rights and self-determination of peoples, and to take other appropriate measures to strengthen universal peace;

3. To achieve international cooperation in solving international problems of an economic, social, cultural, or humanitarian character, and in promoting and encouraging respect for human rights and for fundamental freedoms for all without distinction as to race, sex, language, or religion; and

4. To be a center for harmonizing the actions of nations in the attainment of these common ends.

Article 2

The Organization and its Members, in pursuit of the Purposes stated in Article 1, shall act in accordance with the following Principles.

1. The Organization is based on the principle of the sovereign equality of all its Members.

2. All Members, in order to ensure to all of them the rights and benefits resulting from membership, shall fulfill in good faith the obligations assumed by them in accordance with the present Charter.

3. All Members shall settle their international disputes by peaceful means in such a manner that international peace and security, and justice, are not endangered.

4. All Members shall refrain in their international relations from the threat or use of force against the territorial integrity or political independence of any state, or in any other manner inconsistent with the Purposes of the United Nations.

5. All Members shall give the United Nations every assistance in any action it takes in accordance with the present Charter, and shall refrain from giving assistance to any state against which the United Nations is taking preventive or enforcement action.

6. The Organization shall ensure that states which are not Members of the United Nations act in accordance with these Principles so far as may be necessary for the maintenance of international peace and security.

7. Nothing contained in the present Charter shall authorize the United Nations to intervene in matters which are essentially within the domestic jurisdiction of any state or shall require the Members to submit such matters to settlement under the present Charter; but this principle shall not prejudice the application of enforcement measures under Chapter VII.

...

Chapter IX
International Economic and Social Co-Operation

Article 55

With a view to the creation of conditions of stability and well-being which are necessary for peaceful and friendly relations among nations based on respect for the principle of equal rights and self-determination of peoples, the United Nations shall promote:

a. higher standards of living, full employment, and conditions of economic and social progress and development;

b. solutions of international economic, social, health, and related problems; and international cultural and educational co-operation; and

c. universal respect for, and observance of, human rights and fundamental freedoms for all without distinction as to race, sex, language, or religion.

Article 56

All Members pledge themselves to take joint and separate action in co-
operation with the Organization for the achievement of the purposes set
forth in Article 55.

2.   Universal Declaration of Human Rights

*Adopted and proclaimed by General Assembly resolution 217 A (III) of 10
December 1948.*

On December 10, 1948 the General Assembly of the United Nations
adopted and proclaimed the *Universal Declaration of Human Rights* the
full text of which appears in the following pages. Following this historic
act, the Assembly called upon all member countries to publicize the text
of the U.D.H.R. and "to cause it to be disseminated, displayed, read and
expounded principally in schools and other educational institutions,
without distinction based on the political status of countries or territories".

Preamble

Whereas recognition of the inherent dignity and of the equal and inalienable rights of all members of the human family is the foundation of
freedom, justice and peace in the world,

Whereas disregard and contempt for human rights have resulted in
barbarous acts which have outraged the conscience of mankind, and the
advent of a world in which human beings shall enjoy freedom of speech
and belief and freedom from fear and want has been proclaimed as the
highest aspiration of the common people,

Whereas it is essential, if man is not to be compelled to have recourse, as
a last resort, to rebellion against tyranny and oppression, that human rights
should be protected by the rule of law,

Whereas it is essential to promote the development of friendly relations
between nations,

Whereas the peoples of the United Nations have in the Charter reaffirmed
their faith in fundamental human rights, in the dignity and worth of the
human person and in the equal rights of men and women and have

determined to promote social progress and better standards of life in larger freedom,

Whereas Member States have pledged themselves to achieve, in cooperation with the United Nations, the promotion of universal respect for and observance of human rights and fundamental freedoms,

Whereas a common understanding of these rights and freedoms is of the greatest importance for the full realization of this pledge,

Now, Therefore, The General Assembly proclaims this Universal Declaration of Human Rights as a common standard of achievement for all peoples and all nations, to the end that every individual and every organ of society, keeping this Declaration constantly in mind, shall strive by teaching and education to promote respect for these rights and freedoms and by progressive measures, national and international, to secure their universal and effective recognition and observance, both among the peoples of Member States themselves and among the peoples of territories under their jurisdiction.

Article 1

All human beings are born free and equal in dignity and rights. They are endowed with reason and conscience and should act towards one another in a spirit of brotherhood.

Article 2

Everyone is entitled to all the rights and freedoms set forth in this Declaration, without distinction of any kind, such as race, colour, sex, language, religion, political or other opinion, national or social origin, property, birth or other status.

Furthermore, no distinction shall be made on the basis of the political, jurisdictional or international status of the country or territory to which a person belongs, whether it be independent, trust, non-self-governing or under any other limitation of sovereignty.

Article 3

Everyone has the right to life, liberty and security of person.

Article 4

No one shall be held in slavery or servitude; slavery and the slave trade shall be prohibited in all their forms.

Article 5

No one shall be subjected to torture or to cruel, inhuman or degrading treatment or punishment.

Article 6

Everyone has the right to recognition everywhere as a person before the law.

Article 7

All are equal before the law and are entitled without any discrimination to equal protection of the law. All are entitled to equal protection against any discrimination in violation of this Declaration and against any incitement to such discrimination.

Article 8

Everyone has the right to an effective remedy by the competent national tribunals for acts violating the fundamental rights granted him by the constitution or by law.

Article 9

No one shall be subjected to arbitrary arrest, detention or exile.

Article 10

Everyone is entitled in full equality to a fair and public hearing by an independent and impartial tribunal, in the determination of his rights and obligations and of any criminal charge against him.

Article 11

1. Everyone charged with a penal offence has the right to be presumed innocent until proved guilty according to law in a public trial at which he has had all the guarantees necessary for his defence.

2. No one shall be held guilty of any penal offence on account of any act or omission which did not constitute a penal offence, under national or international law, at the time when it was committed. Nor shall a heavier penalty be imposed than the one that was applicable at the time the penal offence was committed.

Article 12

No one shall be subjected to arbitrary interference with his privacy, family, home or correspondence, nor to attacks upon his honour and reputation. Everyone has the right to the protection of the law against such interference or attacks.

Article 13

1. Everyone has the right to freedom of movement and residence within the borders of each State.

2. Everyone has the right to leave any country, including his own, and to return to his country.

Article 14

1. Everyone has the right to seek and to enjoy in other countries asylum from persecution.

2. This right may not be invoked in the case of prosecutions genuinely arising from non-political crimes or from acts contrary to the purposes and principles of the United Nations.

Article 15

1. Everyone has the right to a nationality.

2. No one shall be arbitrarily deprived of his nationality nor denied the right to change his nationality.

Article 16

1. Men and women of full age, without any limitation due to race, nationality or religion, have the right to marry and to found a family. They are entitled to equal rights as to marriage, during marriage and at its dissolution.

2. Marriage shall be entered into only with the free and full consent of the intending spouses.

3. The family is the natural and fundamental group unit of society and is entitled to protection by society and the State.

Article 17

1. Everyone has the right to own property alone as well as in association with others.

2. No one shall be arbitrarily deprived of his property.

Article 18

Everyone has the right to freedom of thought, conscience and religion; this right includes freedom to change his religion or belief, and freedom, either alone or in community with others and in public or private, to manifest his religion or belief in teaching, practice, worship and observance.

Article 19

Everyone has the right to freedom of opinion and expression; this right includes freedom to hold opinions without interference and to seek, receive and impart information and ideas through any media and regardless of frontiers.

Article 20

1. Everyone has the right to freedom of peaceful assembly and association.

2. No one may be compelled to belong to an association.

Article 21

1. Everyone has the right to take part in the government of his country, directly or through freely chosen representatives.

2. Everyone has the right of equal access to public service in his country.

3. The will of the people shall be the basis of the authority of government; this will shall be expressed in periodic and genuine elections which shall be by universal and equal suffrage and shall be held by secret vote or by equivalent free voting procedures.

Article 22

Everyone, as a member of society, has the right to social security and is entitled to realization, through national effort and international co-operation and in accordance with the organization and resources of each State, of the economic, social and cultural rights indispensable for his dignity and the free development of his personality.

Article 23

1. Everyone has the right to work, to free choice of employment, to just and favourable conditions of work and to protection against unemployment.

2. Everyone, without any discrimination, has the right to equal pay for equal work.

3. Everyone who works has the right to just and favourable remuneration ensuring for himself and his family an existence worthy of human dignity, and supplemented, if necessary, by other means of social protection.

4. Everyone has the right to form and to join trade unions for the protection of his interests.

Article 24

Everyone has the right to rest and leisure, including reasonable limitation of working hours and periodic holidays with pay.

Article 25

1. Everyone has the right to a standard of living adequate for the health and well-being of himself and of his family, including food, clothing, housing and medical care and necessary social services, and the right to security in the event of unemployment, sickness, disability, widowhood, old age or other lack of livelihood in circumstances beyond his control.

2. Motherhood and childhood are entitled to special care and assistance. All children, whether born in or out of wedlock, shall enjoy the same social protection.

Article 26

1. Everyone has the right to education. Education shall be free, at least in the elementary and fundamental stages. Elementary education shall be compulsory. Technical and professional education shall be made generally available and higher education shall be equally accessible to all on the basis of merit.

2. Education shall be directed to the full development of the human personality and to the strengthening of respect for human rights and fundamental freedoms. It shall promote understanding, tolerance and friendship among all nations, racial or religious groups, and shall further the activities of the United Nations for the maintenance of peace.

3. Parents have a prior right to choose the kind of education that shall be given to their children.

Article 27

1. Everyone has the right freely to participate in the cultural life of the community, to enjoy the arts and to share in scientific advancement and its benefits.

2. Everyone has the right to the protection of the moral and material interests resulting from any scientific, literary or artistic production of which he is the author.

Article 28

Everyone is entitled to a social and international order in which the rights and freedoms set forth in this Declaration can be fully realized.

Article 29

1. Everyone has duties to the community in which alone the free and full development of his personality is possible.

2. In the exercise of his rights and freedoms, everyone shall be subject only to such limitations as are determined by law solely for the purpose of securing due recognition and respect for the rights and freedoms of others and of meeting the just requirements of morality, public order and the general welfare in a democratic society.

3. These rights and freedoms may in no case be exercised contrary to the purposes and principles of the United Nations.

Article 30

Nothing in this Declaration may be interpreted as implying for any State, group or person any right to engage in any activity or to perform any act aimed at the destruction of any of the rights and freedoms set forth herein.

3.   International Covenant on Economic, Social and Cultural Rights

G.A. res. 2200A (XXI), 21 U.N. GAOR Supp. (No. 16) at 49, U.N. Doc A/6316 (1966), 993 U.N.T.S. 3, entered into force January 3, 1976.

Preamble

The States Parties to the present Covenant,

Considering that, in accordance with the principles proclaimed in the Charter of the United Nations, recognition of the inherent dignity and of the equal and inalienable rights of all members of the human family is the foundation of freedom, justice and peace in the world,

Recognizing that these rights derive from the inherent dignity of the human person,

Recognizing that, in accordance with the *Universal Declaration of Human Rights*, the ideal of free human beings enjoying freedom from fear and want can only be achieved if conditions are created whereby everyone may enjoy his economic, social and cultural rights, as well as his civil and political rights,

Considering the obligation of States under the Charter of the United Nations to promote universal respect for, and observance of, human rights and freedoms,

Realizing that the individual, having duties to other individuals and to the community to which he belongs, is under a responsibility to strive for the promotion and observance of the rights recognized in the present Covenant,

Agree upon the following articles:

Part I

Article 1

1. All peoples have the right of self-determination. By virtue of that right they freely determine their political status and freely pursue their economic, social and cultural development.

2. All peoples may, for their own ends, freely dispose of their natural wealth and resources without prejudice to any obligations arising out of international economic co-operation, based upon the principle of mutual benefit, and international law. In no case may a people be deprived of its own means of subsistence.

3. The States Parties to the present Covenant, including those having responsibility for the administration of Non-Self-Governing and Trust Territories, shall promote the realization of the right of self-determination, and shall respect that right, in conformity with the provisions of the Charter of the United Nations.

Part II

Article 2

1. Each State Party to the present Covenant undertakes to take steps, individually and through international assistance and co-operation, especially economic and technical, to the maximum of its available resources, with a view to achieving progressively the full realization of the rights recognized in the present Covenant by all appropriate means, including particularly the adoption of legislative measures.

2. The States Parties to the present Covenant undertake to guarantee that the rights enunciated in the present Covenant will be exercised without discrimination of any kind as to race, colour, sex, language, religion, political or other opinion, national or social origin, property, birth or other status.

3. Developing countries, with due regard to human rights and their national economy, may determine to what extent they would guarantee the economic rights recognized in the present Covenant to non-nationals.

Article 3

The States Parties to the present Covenant undertake to ensure the equal right of men and women to the enjoyment of all economic, social and cultural rights set forth in the present Covenant.

Article 4

The States Parties to the present Covenant recognize that, in the enjoyment of those rights provided by the State in conformity with the present Covenant, the State may subject such rights only to such limitations as are determined by law only in so far as this may be compatible with the nature of these rights and solely for the purpose of promoting the general welfare in a democratic society.

Article 5

1. Nothing in the present Covenant may be interpreted as implying for any State, group or person any right to engage in any activity or to perform any act aimed at the destruction of any of the rights or freedoms recognized herein, or at their limitation to a greater extent than is provided for in the present Covenant.

2. No restriction upon or derogation from any of the fundamental human rights recognized or existing in any country in virtue of law, conventions, regulations or custom shall be admitted on the pretext that the present Covenant does not recognize such rights or that it recognizes them to a lesser extent.

Part III

Article 6

1. The States Parties to the present Covenant recognize the right to work, which includes the right of everyone to the opportunity to gain his living by work which he freely chooses or accepts, and will take appropriate steps to safeguard this right.

2. The steps to be taken by a State Party to the present Covenant to achieve the full realization of this right shall include technical and vocational guidance and training programmes, policies and techniques to achieve steady economic, social and cultural development and full and productive employment under conditions safeguarding fundamental political and economic freedoms to the individual.

Article 7

The States Parties to the present Covenant recognize the right of everyone to the enjoyment of just and favourable conditions of work which ensure, in particular:

(a) Remuneration which provides all workers, as a minimum, with:

    (i) Fair wages and equal remuneration for work of equal value without distinction of any kind, in particular women being guaranteed conditions of work not inferior to those enjoyed by men, with equal pay for equal work;

    (ii) A decent living for themselves and their families in accordance with the provisions of the present Covenant;

(b) Safe and healthy working conditions;

(c) Equal opportunity for everyone to be promoted in his employment to an appropriate higher level, subject to no considerations other than those of seniority and competence;

(d) Rest, leisure and reasonable limitation of working hours and periodic holidays with pay, as well as remuneration for public holidays

Article 8

1. The States Parties to the present Covenant undertake to ensure:

(a) The right of everyone to form trade unions and join the trade union of his choice, subject only to the rules of the organization concerned, for the promotion and protection of his economic and social interests. No restrictions may be placed on the exercise of this right other than those prescribed by law and which are necessary in a democratic society in the interests of national security or public order or for the protection of the rights and freedoms of others;

(b) The right of trade unions to establish national federations or confederations and the right of the latter to form or join international trade-union organizations;

(c) The right of trade unions to function freely subject to no limitations other than those prescribed by law and which are necessary in a democratic society in the interests of national security or public order or for the protection of the rights and freedoms of others;

(d) The right to strike, provided that it is exercised in conformity with the laws of the particular country.

2. This article shall not prevent the imposition of lawful restrictions on the exercise of these rights by members of the armed forces or of the police or of the administration of the State.

3. Nothing in this article shall authorize States Parties to the International Labour Organisation Convention of 1948 concerning Freedom of Association and Protection of the Right to Organize to take legislative measures which would prejudice, or apply the law in such a manner as would prejudice, the guarantees provided for in that Convention.

Article 9

The States Parties to the present Covenant recognize the right of everyone to social security, including social insurance.

Article 10

The States Parties to the present Covenant recognize that:

1. The widest possible protection and assistance should be accorded to the family, which is the natural and fundamental group unit of society, particularly for its establishment and while it is responsible for the care and education of dependent children. Marriage must be entered into with the free consent of the intending spouses.

2. Special protection should be accorded to mothers during a reasonable period before and after childbirth. During such period working mothers should be accorded paid leave or leave with adequate social security benefits.

3. Special measures of protection and assistance should be taken on behalf of all children and young persons without any discrimination for reasons of parentage or other conditions. Children and young persons should be protected from economic and social exploitation. Their employment in work harmful to their morals or health or dangerous to life or likely to hamper their normal development should be punishable by law. States should also set age limits below which the paid employment of child labour should be prohibited and punishable by law.

Article 11

1. The States Parties to the present Covenant recognize the right of everyone to an adequate standard of living for himself and his family, including adequate food, clothing and housing, and to the continuous improvement of living conditions. The States Parties will take appropriate steps to ensure the realization of this right, recognizing to this effect the essential importance of international co-operation based on free consent.

2. The States Parties to the present Covenant, recognizing the fundamental right of everyone to be free from hunger, shall take, individually and through international co-operation, the measures, including specific programmes, which are needed:

(a) To improve methods of production, conservation and distribution of food by making full use of technical and scientific knowledge, by disseminating knowledge of the principles of nutrition and by developing or reforming agrarian systems in such a way as to achieve the most efficient development and utilization of natural resources;

(b) Taking into account the problems of both food-importing and food-exporting countries, to ensure an equitable distribution of world food supplies in relation to need.

Article 12

1. The States Parties to the present Covenant recognize the right of everyone to the enjoyment of the highest attainable standard of physical and mental health.

2. The steps to be taken by the States Parties to the present Covenant to achieve the full realization of this right shall include those necessary for:

(a) The provision for the reduction of the stillbirth-rate and of infant mortality and for the healthy development of the child;

(b) The improvement of all aspects of environmental and industrial hygiene;

(c) The prevention, treatment and control of epidemic, endemic, occupational and other diseases;

(d) The creation of conditions which would assure to all medical service and medical attention in the event of sickness.

Article 13

1. The States Parties to the present Covenant recognize the right of everyone to education. They agree that education shall be directed to the

full development of the human personality and the sense of its dignity, and shall strengthen the respect for human rights and fundamental freedoms. They further agree that education shall enable all persons to participate effectively in a free society, promote understanding, tolerance and friendship among all nations and all racial, ethnic or religious groups, and further the activities of the United Nations for the maintenance of peace.

2. The States Parties to the present Covenant recognize that, with a view to achieving the full realization of this right:

(a) Primary education shall be compulsory and available free to all;

(b) Secondary education in its different forms, including technical and vocational secondary education, shall be made generally available and accessible to all by every appropriate means, and in particular by the progressive introduction of free education;

(c) Higher education shall be made equally accessible to all, on the basis of capacity, by every appropriate means, and in particular by the progressive introduction of free education;

(d) Fundamental education shall be encouraged or intensified as far as possible for those persons who have not received or completed the whole period of their primary education;

(e) The development of a system of schools at all levels shall be actively pursued, an adequate fellowship system shall be established, and the material conditions of teaching staff shall be continuously improved.

3. The States Parties to the present Covenant undertake to have respect for the liberty of parents and, when applicable, legal guardians to choose for their children schools, other than those established by the public authorities, which conform to such minimum educational standards as may be laid down or approved by the State and to ensure the religious and moral education of their children in conformity with their own convictions.

4. No part of this article shall be construed so as to interfere with the liberty of individuals and bodies to establish and direct educational institutions, subject always to the observance of the principles set forth in paragraph I of this article and to the requirement that the education given in such institutions shall conform to such minimum standards as may be laid down by the State.

Article 14

Each State Party to the present Covenant which, at the time of becoming a Party, has not been able to secure in its metropolitan territory or other territories under its jurisdiction compulsory primary education, free of charge, undertakes, within two years, to work out and adopt a detailed plan of action for the progressive implementation, within a reasonable number of years, to be fixed in the plan, of the principle of compulsory education free of charge for all.

Article 15

1. The States Parties to the present Covenant recognize the right of everyone:

    (a) To take part in cultural life;

    (b) To enjoy the benefits of scientific progress and its applications;

    (c) To benefit from the protection of the moral and material interests resulting from any scientific, literary or artistic production of which he is the author.

2. The steps to be taken by the States Parties to the present Covenant to achieve the full realization of this right shall include those necessary for the conservation, the development and the diffusion of science and culture.

3. The States Parties to the present Covenant undertake to respect the freedom indispensable for scientific research and creative activity.

4. The States Parties to the present Covenant recognize the benefits to be derived from the encouragement and development of international contacts and co-operation in the scientific and cultural fields.

Articles 16 - 27 omitted

Article 28

The provisions of the present Covenant shall extend to all parts of federal States without any limitations or exceptions.

Articles 29 - 31 omitted

4.   International Covenant on Civil and Political Rights

G.A. res. 2200A (XXI), 21 U.N. GAOR Supp. (No. 16) at 52, U.N. Doc. A/6316 (1966), 999 U.N.T.S. 171, entered into force Mar. 23, 1976.

Preamble

The States Parties to the present Covenant,

Considering that, in accordance with the principles proclaimed in the Charter of the United Nations, recognition of the inherent dignity and of the equal and inalienable rights of all members of the human family is the foundation of freedom, justice and peace in the world,

Recognizing that these rights derive from the inherent dignity of the human person,

Recognizing that, in accordance with the Universal Declaration of Human Rights, the ideal of free human beings enjoying civil and political freedom and freedom from fear and want can only be achieved if conditions are created whereby everyone may enjoy his civil and political rights, as well as his economic, social and cultural rights,

Considering the obligation of States under the Charter of the United Nations to promote universal respect for, and observance of, human rights and freedoms,

Realizing that the individual, having duties to other individuals and to the community to which he belongs, is under a responsibility to strive for the promotion and observance of the rights recognized in the present Covenant,

Agree upon the following articles:

Part I

Article I

1. All peoples have the right of self-determination. By virtue of that right they freely determine their political status and freely pursue their economic, social and cultural development.

2. All peoples may, for their own ends, freely dispose of their natural wealth and resources without prejudice to any obligations arising out of international economic co-operation, based upon the principle of mutual benefit, and international law. In no case may a people be deprived of its own means of subsistence.

3. The States Parties to the present Covenant, including those having responsibility for the administration of Non-Self-Governing and Trust Territories, shall promote the realization of the right of self-determination, and shall respect that right, in conformity with the provisions of the Charter of the United Nations.

Part II

Article 2

1. Each State Party to the present Covenant undertakes to respect and to ensure to all individuals within its territory and subject to its jurisdiction the rights recognized in the present Covenant, without distinction of any kind, such as race, colour, sex, language, religion, political or other opinion, national or social origin, property, birth or other status.

2. Where not already provided for by existing legislative or other measures, each State Party to the present Covenant undertakes to take the necessary steps, in accordance with its constitutional processes and with the provisions of the present Covenant, to adopt such legislative or other measures as may be necessary to give effect to the rights recognized in the present Covenant.

3. Each State Party to the present Covenant undertakes:

   (a) To ensure that any person whose rights or freedoms as herein recognized are violated shall have an effective remedy, notwithstanding that the violation has been committed by persons acting in an official capacity;

   (b) To ensure that any person claiming such a remedy shall have his right thereto determined by competent judicial, administrative or legislative authorities, or by any other competent authority provided for by the legal system of the State, and to develop the possibilities of judicial remedy;

   (c) To ensure that the competent authorities shall enforce such remedies when granted.

Article 3

The States Parties to the present Covenant undertake to ensure the equal right of men and women to the enjoyment of all civil and political rights set forth in the present Covenant.

Article 4

1. In time of public emergency which threatens the life of the nation and the existence of which is officially proclaimed, the States Parties to the present Covenant may take measures derogating from their obligations under the present Covenant to the extent strictly required by the exigencies of the situation, provided that such measures are not inconsistent with their other obligations under international law and do not involve dis-

crimination solely on the ground of race, colour, sex, language, religion or social origin.

2. No derogation from articles 6, 7, 8 (paragraphs I and 2), 11, 15, 16 and 18 may be made under this provision.

3. Any State Party to the present Covenant availing itself of the right of derogation shall immediately inform the other States Parties to the present Covenant, through the intermediary of the Secretary-General of the United Nations, of the provisions from which it has derogated and of the reasons by which it was actuated. A further communication shall be made, through the same intermediary, on the date on which it terminates such derogation.

Article 5

1. Nothing in the present Covenant may be interpreted as implying for any State, group or person any right to engage in any activity or perform any act aimed at the destruction of any of the rights and freedoms recognized herein or at their limitation to a greater extent than is provided for in the present Covenant.

2. There shall be no restriction upon or derogation from any of the fundamental human rights recognized or existing in any State Party to the present Covenant pursuant to law, conventions, regulations or custom on the pretext that the present Covenant does not recognize such rights or that it recognizes them to a lesser extent.

Part III

Article 6

1. Every human being has the inherent right to life. This right shall be protected by law. No one shall be arbitrarily deprived of his life.

2. In countries which have not abolished the death penalty, sentence of death may be imposed only for the most serious crimes in accordance with the law in force at the time of the commission of the crime and not contrary to the provisions of the present Covenant and to the Convention on the Prevention and Punishment of the Crime of Genocide. This penalty can only be carried out pursuant to a final judgement rendered by a competent court.

3. When deprivation of life constitutes the crime of genocide, it is understood that nothing in this article shall authorize any State Party to the present Covenant to derogate in any way from any obligation assumed

under the provisions of the Convention on the Prevention and Punishment of the Crime of Genocide.

4. Anyone sentenced to death shall have the right to seek pardon or commutation of the sentence. Amnesty, pardon or commutation of the sentence of death may be granted in all cases.

5. Sentence of death shall not be imposed for crimes committed by persons below eighteen years of age and shall not be carried out on pregnant women.

6. Nothing in this article shall be invoked to delay or to prevent the abolition of capital punishment by any State Party to the present Covenant.

Article 7

No one shall be subjected to torture or to cruel, inhuman or degrading treatment or punishment. In particular, no one shall be subjected without his free consent to medical or scientific experimentation.

Article 8

1. No one shall be held in slavery; slavery and the slave-trade in all their forms shall be prohibited.

2. No one shall be held in servitude.

3. (a) No one shall be required to perform forced or compulsory labour;

   (b) Paragraph 3 (a) shall not be held to preclude, in countries where imprisonment with hard labour may be imposed as a punishment for a crime, the performance of hard labour in pursuance of a sentence to such punishment by a competent court;

   (c) For the purpose of this paragraph the term "forced or compulsory labour" shall not include:

      (i)   Any work or service, not referred to in subparagraph (b), normally required of a person who is under detention in consequence of a lawful order of a court, or of a person during conditional release from such detention;

      (ii) Any service of a military character and, in countries where conscientious objection is recognized, any national service required by law of conscientious objectors;

      (iii) Any service exacted in cases of emergency or calamity threatening the life or well-being of the community;

      (iv) Any work or service which forms part of normal civil obligations.

Article 9

1. Everyone has the right to liberty and security of person. No one shall be subjected to arbitrary arrest or detention. No one shall be deprived of his liberty except on such grounds and in accordance with such procedure as are established by law.

2. Anyone who is arrested shall be informed, at the time of arrest, of the reasons for his arrest and shall be promptly informed of any charges against him.

3. Anyone arrested or detained on a criminal charge shall be brought promptly before a judge or other officer authorized by law to exercise judicial power and shall be entitled to trial within a reasonable time or to release. It shall not be the general rule that persons awaiting trial shall be detained in custody, but release may be subject to guarantees to appear for trial, at any other stage of the judicial proceedings, and, should occasion arise, for execution of the judgement.

4. Anyone who is deprived of his liberty by arrest or detention shall be entitled to take proceedings before a court, in order that court may decide without delay on the lawfulness of his detention and order his release if the detention is not lawful.

5. Anyone who has been the victim of unlawful arrest or detention shall have an enforceable right to compensation.

Article 10

1. All persons deprived of their liberty shall be treated with humanity and with respect for the inherent dignity of the human person.

2. (a) Accused persons shall, save in exceptional circumstances, be segregated from convicted persons and shall be subject to separate treatment appropriate to their status as unconvicted persons;

   (b) Accused juvenile persons shall be separated from adults and brought as speedily as possible for adjudication.

3. The penitentiary system shall comprise treatment of prisoners the essential aim of which shall be their reformation and social rehabilitation. Juvenile offenders shall be segregated from adults and be accorded treatment appropriate to their age and legal status.

Article 11

No one shall be imprisoned merely on the ground of inability to fulfil a contractual obligation.

Article 12

1. Everyone lawfully within the territory of a State shall, within that territory, have the right to liberty of movement and freedom to choose his residence.

2. Everyone shall be free to leave any country, including his own.

3. The above-mentioned rights shall not be subject to any restrictions except those which are provided by law, are necessary to protect national security, public order (ordre public), public health or morals or the rights and freedoms of others, and are consistent with the other rights recognized in the present Covenant.

4. No one shall be arbitrarily deprived of the right to enter his own country.

Article 13

An alien lawfully in the territory of a State Party to the present Covenant may be expelled therefrom only in pursuance of a decision reached in accordance with law and shall, except where compelling reasons of national security otherwise require, be allowed to submit the reasons against his expulsion and to have his case reviewed by, and be represented for the purpose before, the competent authority or a person or persons especially designated by the competent authority.

Article 14

1. All persons shall be equal before the courts and tribunals. In the determination of any criminal charge against him, or of his rights and obligations in a suit at law, everyone shall be entitled to a fair and public hearing by a competent, independent and impartial tribunal established by law. The press and the public may be excluded from all or part of a trial for reasons of morals, public order (ordre public) or national security in a democratic society, or when the interest of the private lives of the parties so requires, or to the extent strictly necessary in the opinion of the court in special circumstances where publicity would prejudice the interests of justice; but any judgement rendered in a criminal case or in a suit at law shall be made public except where the interest of juvenile persons otherwise requires or the proceedings concern matrimonial disputes or the guardianship of children.

2. Everyone charged with a criminal offence shall have the right to be presumed innocent until proved guilty according to law.

3. In the determination of any criminal charge against him, everyone shall be entitled to the following minimum guarantees, in full equality:

(a) To be informed promptly and in detail in a language which he understands of the nature and cause of the charge against him;

(b) To have adequate time and facilities for the preparation of his defence and to communicate with counsel of his own choosing;

(c) To be tried without undue delay;

(d) To be tried in his presence, and to defend himself in person or through legal assistance of his own choosing; to be informed, if he does not have legal assistance, of this right; and to have legal assistance assigned to him, in any case where the interests of justice so require, and without payment by him in any such case if he does not have sufficient means to pay for it;

(e) To examine, or have examined, the witnesses against him and to obtain the attendance and examination of witnesses on his behalf under the same conditions as witnesses against him;

(f) To have the free assistance of an interpreter if he cannot understand or speak the language used in court;

(g) Not to be compelled to testify against himself or to confess guilt.

4. In the case of juvenile persons, the procedure shall be such as will take account of their age and the desirability of promoting their rehabilitation.

5. Everyone convicted of a crime shall have the right to his conviction and sentence being reviewed by a higher tribunal according to law.

6. When a person has by a final decision been convicted of a criminal offence and when subsequently his conviction has been reversed or he has been pardoned on the ground that a new or newly discovered fact shows conclusively that there has been a miscarriage of justice, the person who has suffered punishment as a result of such conviction shall be compensated according to law, unless it is proved that the non-disclosure of the unknown fact in time is wholly or partly attributable to him.

7. No one shall be liable to be tried or punished again for an offence for which he has already been finally convicted or acquitted in accordance with the law and penal procedure of each country.

Article 15

1. No one shall be held guilty of any criminal offence on account of any act or omission which did not constitute a criminal offence, under national or international law, at the time when it was committed. Nor shall a heavier penalty be imposed than the one that was applicable at the time when the criminal offence was committed. If, subsequent to the commission

of the offence, provision is made by law for the imposition of the lighter penalty, the offender shall benefit thereby.

2. Nothing in this article shall prejudice the trial and punishment of any person for any act or omission which, at the time when it was committed, was criminal according to the general principles of law recognized by the community of nations.

Article 16

Everyone shall have the right to recognition everywhere as a person before the law.

Article 17

1. No one shall be subjected to arbitrary or unlawful interference with his privacy, family, home or correspondence, nor to unlawful attacks on his honour and reputation.

2. Everyone has the right to the protection of the law against such interference or attacks.

Article 18

1. Everyone shall have the right to freedom of thought, conscience and religion. This right shall include freedom to have or to adopt a religion or belief of his choice, and freedom, either individually or in community with others and in public or private, to manifest his religion or belief in worship, observance, practice and teaching.

2. No one shall be subject to coercion which would impair his freedom to have or to adopt a religion or belief of his choice.

3. Freedom to manifest one's religion or beliefs may be subject only to such limitations as are prescribed by law and are necessary to protect public safety, order, health, or morals or the fundamental rights and freedoms of others.

4. The States Parties to the present Covenant undertake to have respect for the liberty of parents and, when applicable, legal guardians to ensure the religious and moral education of their children in conformity with their own convictions.

Article 19

1. Everyone shall have the right to hold opinions without interference.

2. Everyone shall have the right to freedom of expression; this right shall include freedom to seek, receive and impart information and ideas of all

kinds, regardless of frontiers, either orally, in writing or in print, in the form of art, or through any other media of his choice.

3. The exercise of the rights provided for in paragraph 2 of this article carries with it special duties and responsibilities. It may therefore be subject to certain restrictions, but these shall only be such as are provided by law and are necessary:

(a) For respect of the rights or reputations of others;

(b) For the protection of national security or of public order (ordre public), or of public health or morals.

Article 20

1. Any propaganda for war shall be prohibited by law.

2. Any advocacy of national, racial or religious hatred that constitutes incitement to discrimination, hostility or violence shall be prohibited by law.

Article 21

The right of peaceful assembly shall be recognized. No restrictions may be placed on the exercise of this right other than those imposed in conformity with the law and which are necessary in a democratic society in the interests of national security or public safety, public order (ordre public), the protection of public health or morals or the protection of the rights and freedoms of others.

Article 22

1. Everyone shall have the right to freedom of association with others, including the right to form and join trade unions for the protection of his interests.

2. No restrictions may be placed on the exercise of this right other than those which are prescribed by law and which are necessary in a democratic society in the interests of national security or public safety, public order (ordre public), the protection of public health or morals or the protection of the rights and freedoms of others. This article shall not prevent the imposition of lawful restrictions on members of the armed forces and of the police in their exercise of this right.

3. Nothing in this article shall authorize States Parties to the International Labour Organisation Convention of 1948 concerning Freedom of Association and Protection of the Right to Organize to take legislative measures which would prejudice, or to apply the law in such a manner as to prejudice, the guarantees provided for in that Convention.

Article 23

1. The family is the natural and fundamental group unit of society and is entitled to protection by society and the State.

2. The right of men and women of marriageable age to marry and to found a family shall be recognized.

3. No marriage shall be entered into without the free and full consent of the intending spouses.

4. States Parties to the present Covenant shall take appropriate steps to ensure equality of rights and responsibilities of spouses as to marriage, during marriage and at its dissolution. In the case of dissolution, provision shall be made for the necessary protection of any children.

Article 24

1. Every child shall have, without any discrimination as to race, colour, sex, language, religion, national or social origin, property or birth, the right to such measures of protection as are required by his status as a minor, on the part of his family, society and the State.

2. Every child shall be registered immediately after birth and shall have a name.

3. Every child has the right to acquire a nationality.

Article 25

Every citizen shall have the right and the opportunity, without any of the distinctions mentioned in article 2 and without unreasonable restrictions:

    (a) To take part in the conduct of public affairs, directly or through freely chosen representatives;

    (b) To vote and to be elected at genuine periodic elections which shall be by universal and equal suffrage and shall be held by secret ballot, guaranteeing the free expression of the will of the electors;

    (c) To have access, on general terms of equality, to public service in his country.

Article 26

All persons are equal before the law and are entitled without any discrimination to the equal protection of the law. In this respect, the law shall prohibit any discrimination and guarantee to all persons equal and effective protection against discrimination on any ground such as race, colour, sex, language, religion, political or other opinion, national or social origin, property, birth or other status.

Article 27

In those States in which ethnic, religious or linguistic minorities exist, persons belonging to such minorities shall not be denied the right, in community with the other members of their group, to enjoy their own culture, to profess and practise their own religion, or to use their own language.

Articles 28 - 49 omitted

Article 50

The provisions of the present Covenant shall extend to all parts of federal States without any limitations or exceptions.

Articles 51 - 53 omitted

5.   International Convention on the Elimination of All Forms of Racial Discrimination

G.A. Res. 2106 (XX), Annex, 20 U.N. GAOR Supp. (No. 14) at 47, U.N. Doc. A/6014 (1966), 660 U.N.T.S. 195, entered into force Jan. 4, 1969.

The States Parties to this Convention,

Considering that the Charter of the United Nations is based on the principles of the dignity and equality inherent in all human beings, and that all Member States have pledged themselves to take joint and separate action, in co-operation with the Organization, for the achievement of one of the purposes of the United Nations which is to promote and encourage universal respect for and observance of human rights and fundamental freedoms for all, without distinction as to race, sex, language or religion,

Considering that the Universal Declaration of Human Rights proclaims that all human beings are born free and equal in dignity and rights and that everyone is entitled to all the rights and freedoms set out therein, without distinction of any kind, in particular as to race, colour or national origin,

Considering that all human beings are equal before the law and are entitled to equal protection of the law against any discrimination and against any incitement to discrimination,

Considering that the United Nations has condemned colonialism and all practices of segregation and discrimination associated therewith, in whatever form and wherever they exist, and that the Declaration on the Granting of Independence to Colonial Countries and Peoples of 14 December 1960 (General Assembly Resolution 1514 (XV)) has affirmed and solemnly proclaimed the necessity of bringing them to a speedy and unconditional end,

Considering that the United Nations Declaration on the Elimination of All Forms of Racial Discrimination of 20 November 1963 (General Assembly resolution 1904 (XVIII)) solemnly affirms the necessity of speedily eliminating racial discrimination throughout the world in all its forms and manifestations and of securing understanding of and respect for the dignity of the human person,

Convinced that any doctrine of superiority based on racial differentiation is scientifically false, morally condemnable, socially unjust and dangerous, and that there is no justification for racial discrimination, in theory or in practice, anywhere,

Reaffirming that discrimination between human beings on the grounds of race, colour or ethnic origin is an obstacle to friendly and peaceful relations among nations and is capable of disturbing peace and security among peoples and the harmony of persons living side by side even within one and the same State,

Convinced that the existence of racial barriers is repugnant to the ideals of any human society,

Alarmed by manifestations of racial discrimination still in evidence in some areas of the world and by governmental policies based on racial superiority or hatred, such as policies of apartheid, segregation or separation,

Resolved to adopt all necessary measures for speedily eliminating racial discrimination in all its forms and manifestations, and to prevent and combat racist doctrines and practices in order to promote understanding between races and to build an international community free from all forms of racial segregation and racial discrimination,

Bearing in mind the Convention concerning Discrimination in respect of Employment and Occupation adopted by the International Labour Organisation in 1958, and the Convention against Discrimination in Education adopted by the United Nations Educational, Scientific and Cultural Organization in 1960,

Desiring to implement the principles embodied in the United Nations Declaration on the Elimination of Al l Forms of Racial Discrimination and to secure the earliest adoption of practical measures to that end,

Have agreed as follows:

Part I

Article 1

1. In this Convention, the term "racial discrimination" shall mean any distinction, exclusion, restriction or preference based on race, colour, descent, or national or ethnic origin which has the purpose or effect of nullifying or impairing the recognition, enjoyment or exercise, on an equal footing, of human rights and fundamental freedoms in the political, economic, social, cultural or any other field of public life.

2. This Convention shall not apply to distinctions, exclusions, restrictions or preferences made by a State Party to this Convention between citizens and non-citizens.

3. Nothing in this Convention may be interpreted as affecting in any way the legal provisions of States Parties concerning nationality, citizenship or naturalization, provided that such provisions do not discriminate against any particular nationality.

4. Special measures taken for the sole purpose of securing adequate advancement of certain racial or ethnic groups or individuals requiring such protection as may be necessary in order to ensure such groups or individuals equal enjoyment or exercise of human rights and fundamental freedoms shall not be deemed racial discrimination, provided, however, that such measures do not, as a consequence, lead to the maintenance of separate rights for different racial groups and that they shall not be continued after the objectives for which they were taken have been achieved.

Article 2

1. States Parties condemn racial discrimination and undertake to pursue by all appropriate means and without delay a policy of eliminating racial discrimination in all its forms and promoting understanding among all races, and, to this end:

   (a) Each State Party undertakes to engage in no act or practice of racial discrimination against persons, groups of persons or institutions and to ensure that all public authorities and public institutions, national and local, shall act in conformity with this obligation;

(b) Each State Party undertakes not to sponsor, defend or support racial discrimination by any persons or organizations;

(c) Each State Party shall take effective measures to review governmental, national and local policies, and to amend, rescind or nullify any laws and regulations which have the effect of creating or perpetuating racial discrimination wherever it exists;

(d) Each State Party shall prohibit and bring to an end, by all appropriate means, including legislation as required by circumstances, racial discrimination by any persons, group or organization;

(e) Each State Party undertakes to encourage, where appropriate, integrationist multiracial organizations and movements and other means of eliminating barriers between races, and to discourage anything which tends to strengthen racial division.

2. States Parties shall, when the circumstances so warrant, take, in the social, economic, cultural and other fields, special and concrete measures to ensure the adequate development and protection of certain racial groups or individuals belonging to them, for the purpose of guaranteeing them the full and equal enjoyment of human rights and fundamental freedoms. These measures shall in no case entail as a consequence the maintenance of unequal or separate rights for different racial groups after the objectives for which they were taken have been achieved.

Article 3

States Parties particularly condemn racial segregation and apartheid and undertake to prevent, prohibit and eradicate all practices of this nature in territories under their jurisdiction.

Article 4

States Parties condemn all propaganda and all organizations which are based on ideas or theories of superiority of one race or group of persons of one colour or ethnic origin, or which attempt to justify or promote racial hatred and discrimination in any form, and undertake to adopt immediate and positive measures designed to eradicate all incitement to, or acts of, such discrimination and, to this end, with due regard to the principles embodied in the Universal Declaration of Human Rights and the rights expressly set forth in article 5 of this Convention, inter alia:

(a) Shall declare an offence punishable by law all dissemination of ideas based on racial superiority or hatred, incitement to racial discrimination, as well as all acts of violence or incitement to such acts against any race or group of persons of another colour or ethnic origin, and also the provision of any assistance to racist activities, including the financing thereof;

(b) Shall declare illegal and prohibit organizations, and also organized and all other propaganda activities, which promote and incite racial discrimination, and shall recognize participation in such organizations or activities as an offence punishable by law;

(c) Shall not permit public authorities or public institutions, national or local, to promote or incite racial discrimination.

Article 5

In compliance with the fundamental obligations laid down in article 2 of this Convention, States Parties undertake to prohibit and to eliminate racial discrimination in all its forms and to guarantee the right of everyone, without distinction as to race, colour, or national or ethnic origin, to equality before the law, notably in the enjoyment of the following rights:

(a) The right to equal treatment before the tribunals and all other organs administering justice;

(b) The right to security of person and protection by the State against violence or bodily harm, whether inflicted by government officials or by any individual group or institution;

(c) Political rights, in particular the right to participate in elections-to vote and to stand for election-on the basis of universal and equal suffrage, to take part in the Government as well as in the conduct of public affairs at any level and to have equal access to public service;

(d) Other civil rights, in particular:

   (i)   The right to freedom of movement and residence within the border of the State;

   (ii)   The right to leave any country, including one's own, and to return to one's country;

   (iii) The right to nationality;

   (iv)   The right to marriage and choice of spouse;

   (v)   The right to own property alone as well as in association with others;

   (vi)   The right to inherit;

    (vii) The right to freedom of thought, conscience and religion;

    (viii) The right to freedom of opinion and expression;

    (ix)   The right to freedom of peaceful assembly and association;

  (e) Economic, social and cultural rights, in particular:

    (i)   The rights to work, to free choice of employment, to just and favourable conditions of work, to protection against unemployment, to equal pay for equal work, to just and favourable remuneration;

    (ii)   The right to form and join trade unions;

    (iii) The right to housing;

    (iv) The right to public health, medical care, social security and social services;

    (v)   The right to education and training;

    (vi) The right to equal participation in cultural activities;

  (f) The right of access to any place or service intended for use by the general public, such as transport, hotels, restaurants, cafés, theatres and parks.

Article 6

States Parties shall assure to everyone within their jurisdiction effective protection and remedies, through the competent national tribunals and other State institutions, against any acts of racial discrimination which violate his human rights and fundamental freedoms contrary to this Convention, as well as the right to seek from such tribunals just and adequate reparation or satisfaction for any damage suffered as a result of such discrimination.

Article 7

States Parties undertake to adopt immediate and effective measures, particularly in the fields of teaching, education, culture and information, with a view to combating prejudices which lead to racial discrimination and to promoting understanding, tolerance and friendship among nations and racial or ethnical groups, as well as to propagating the purposes and principles of the Charter of the United Nations, the Universal Declaration of Human Rights, the United Nations Declaration on the Elimination of All Forms of Racial Discrimination, and this Convention.

6.   Convention on the Elimination of All Forms of Discrimination against Women

G.A. Res. 34/180, 34 U.N. GAOR Supp. (No. 46) at 193, U.N. Doc. A/34/46, entered into force Sept. 3, 1981.

The States Parties to the present Convention,

Noting that the Charter of the United Nations reaffirms faith in fundamental human rights, in the dignity and worth of the human person and in the equal rights of men and women,

Noting that the Universal Declaration of Human Rights affirms the principle of the inadmissibility of discrimination and proclaims that all human beings are born free and equal in dignity and rights and that everyone is entitled to all the rights and freedoms set forth therein, without distinction of any kind, including distinction based on sex,

Noting that the States Parties to the International Covenants on Human Rights have the obligation to ensure the equal rights of men and women to enjoy all economic, social, cultural, civil and political rights,

Considering the international conventions concluded under the auspices of the United Nations and the specialized agencies promoting equality of rights of men and women,

Noting also the resolutions, declarations and recommendations adopted by the United Nations and the specialized agencies promoting equality of rights of men and women,

Concerned, however, that despite these various instruments extensive discrimination against women continues to exist,

Recalling that discrimination against women violates the principles of equality of rights and respect for human dignity, is an obstacle to the participation of women, on equal terms with men, in the political, social, economic and cultural life of their countries, hampers the growth of the prosperity of society and the family and makes more difficult the full development of the potentialities of women in the service of their countries and of humanity,

Concerned that in situations of poverty women have the least access to food, health, education, training and opportunities for employment and other needs,

Convinced that the establishment of the new international economic order based on equity and justice will contribute significantly towards the promotion of equality between men and women,

Emphasizing that the eradication of apartheid, all forms of racism, racial discrimination, colonialism, neo-colonialism, aggression, foreign occupation and domination and interference in the internal affairs of States is essential to the full enjoyment of the rights of men and women,

Affirming that the strengthening of international peace and security, the relaxation of international tension, mutual co-operation among all States irrespective of their social and economic systems, general and complete disarmament, in particular nuclear disarmament under strict and effective international control, the affirmation of the principles of justice, equality and mutual benefit in relations among countries and the realization of the right of peoples under alien and colonial domination and foreign occupation to self-determination and independence, as well as respect for national sovereignty and territorial integrity, will promote social progress and development and as a consequence will contribute to the attainment of full equality between men and women,

Convinced that the full and complete development of a country, the welfare of the world and the cause of peace require the maximum participation of women on equal terms with men in all fields,

Bearing in mind the great contribution of women to the welfare of the family and to the development of society, so far not fully recognized, the social significance of maternity and the role of both parents in the family and in the upbringing of children, and aware that the role of women in procreation should not be a basis for discrimination but that the upbringing of children requires a sharing of responsibility between men and women and society as a whole,

Aware that a change in the traditional role of men as well as the role of women in society and in the family is needed to achieve full equality between men and women,

Determined to implement the principles set forth in the Declaration on the Elimination of Discrimination against Women and, for that purpose, to adopt the measures required for the elimination of such discrimination in all its forms and manifestations,

Have agreed on the following:

Part I

Article 1

For the purposes of the present Convention, the term "discrimination against women" shall mean any distinction, exclusion or restriction made on the basis of sex which has the effect or purpose of impairing or nullifying the recognition, enjoyment or exercise by women, irrespective of their marital status, on a basis of equality of men and women, of human rights and fundamental freedoms in the political, economic, social, cultural, civil or any other field.

Article 2

States Parties condemn discrimination against women in all its forms, agree to pursue by all appropriate means and without delay a policy of eliminating discrimination against women and, to this end, undertake:

(a) To embody the principle of the equality of men and women in their national constitutions or other appropriate legislation if not yet incorporated therein and to ensure, through law and other appropriate means, the practical realization of this principle;

(b) To adopt appropriate legislative and other measures, including sanctions where appropriate, prohibiting all discrimination against women;

(c) To establish legal protection of the rights of women on an equal basis with men and to ensure through competent national tribunals and other public institutions the effective protection of women against any act of discrimination;

(d) To refrain from engaging in any act or practice of discrimination against women and to ensure that public authorities and institutions shall act in conformity with this obligation;

(e) To take all appropriate measures to eliminate discrimination against women by any person, organization or enterprise;

(f) To take all appropriate measures, including legislation, to modify or abolish existing laws, regulations, customs and practices which constitute discrimination against women;

(g) To repeal all national penal provisions which constitute discrimination against women.

Article 3

States Parties shall take in all fields, in particular in the political, social, economic and cultural fields, all appropriate measures, including legislation, to ensure the full development and advancement of women, for the purpose of guaranteeing them the exercise and enjoyment of human rights and fundamental freedoms on a basis of equality with men.

Article 4

1. Adoption by States Parties of temporary special measures aimed at accelerating de facto equality between men and women shall not be considered discrimination as defined in the present Convention, but shall in no way entail as a consequence the maintenance of unequal or separate standards; these measures shall be discontinued when the objectives of equality of opportunity and treatment have been achieved.

2. Adoption by States Parties of special measures, including those measures contained in the present Convention, aimed at protecting maternity shall not be considered discriminatory.

Article 5

States Parties shall take all appropriate measures:

(a) To modify the social and cultural patterns of conduct of men and women, with a view to achieving the elimination of prejudices and customary and all other practices which are based on the idea of the inferiority or the superiority of either of the sexes or on stereotyped roles for men and women;

(b) To ensure that family education includes a proper understanding of maternity as a social function and the recognition of the common responsibility of men and women in the upbringing and development of their children, it being understood that the interest of the children is the primordial consideration in all cases.

Article 6

States Parties shall take all appropriate measures, including legislation, to suppress all forms of traffic in women and exploitation of prostitution of women.

7. Convention on the Rights of the Child

G.A. res. 44/25, Annex, 44 U.N. GAOR Supp. (No. 49) at 167, U.N. Doc. A/44/49 (1989), entered into force Sept. 2 1990.

Preamble

The States Parties to the present Convention,

Considering that, in accordance with the principles proclaimed in the Charter of the United Nations, recognition of the inherent dignity and of the equal and inalienable rights of all members of the human family is the foundation of freedom, justice and peace in the world,

Bearing in mind that the peoples of the United Nations have, in the Charter, reaffirmed their faith in fundamental human rights and in the dignity and worth of the human person, and have determined to promote social progress and better standards of life in larger freedom,

Recognizing that the United Nations has, in the Universal Declaration of Human Rights and in the International Covenants on Human Rights, proclaimed and agreed that everyone is entitled to all the rights and freedoms set forth therein, without distinction of any kind, such as race, colour, sex, language, religion, political or other opinion, national or social origin, property, birth or other status,

Recalling that, in the Universal Declaration of Human Rights, the United Nations has proclaimed that childhood is entitled to special care and assistance,

Convinced that the family, as the fundamental group of society and the natural environment for the growth and well-being of all its members and particularly children, should be afforded the necessary protection and assistance so that it can fully assume its responsibilities within the community,

Recognizing that the child, for the full and harmonious development of his or her personality, should grow up in a family environment, in an atmosphere of happiness, love and understanding,

Considering that the child should be fully prepared to live an individual life in society, and brought up in the spirit of the ideals proclaimed in the Charter of the United Nations, and in particular in the spirit of peace, dignity, tolerance, freedom, equality and solidarity,

Bearing in mind that the need to extend particular care to the child has been stated in the Geneva Declaration of the Rights of the Child of 1924 and in the Declaration of the Rights of the Child adopted by the General Assembly on 20 November 1959 and recognized in the Universal Declaration of Human Rights, in the International Covenant on Civil and Political Rights (in particular in articles 23 and 24), in the International Covenant on Economic, Social and Cultural Rights (in particular in article 10) and in the statutes and relevant instruments of specialized agencies and international organizations concerned with the welfare of children,

Bearing in mind that, as indicated in the Declaration of the Rights of the Child, "the child, by reason of his physical and mental immaturity, needs special safeguards and care, including appropriate legal protection, before as well as after birth",

Recalling the provisions of the Declaration on Social and Legal Principles relating to the Protection and Welfare of Children, with Special Reference to Foster Placement and Adoption Nationally and Internationally; the United Nations Standard Minimum Rules for the Administration of Juvenile Justice (The Beijing Rules); and the Declaration on the Protection of Women and Children in Emergency and Armed Conflict,

Recognizing that, in all countries in the world, there are children living in exceptionally difficult conditions, and that such children need special consideration,

Taking due account of the importance of the traditions and cultural values of each people for the protection and harmonious development of the child,

Recognizing the importance of international co-operation for improving the living conditions of children in every country, in particular in the developing countries,

Have agreed as follows:

Part I

Article 1

For the purposes of the present Convention, a child means every human being below the age of eighteen years unless under the law applicable to the child, majority is attained earlier.

Article 2

1. States Parties shall respect and ensure the rights set forth in the present Convention to each child within their jurisdiction without discrimination of any kind, irrespective of the child's or his or her parent's or legal guardian's race, colour, sex, language, religion, political or other opinion, national, ethnic or social origin, property, disability, birth or other status.

2. States Parties shall take all appropriate measures to ensure that the child is protected against all forms of discrimination or punishment on the basis of the status, activities, expressed opinions, or beliefs of the child's parents, legal guardians, or family members.

Article 3

1. In all actions concerning children, whether undertaken by public or private social welfare institutions, courts of law, administrative authorities or legislative bodies, the best interests of the child shall be a primary consideration.

2. States Parties undertake to ensure the child such protection and care as is necessary for his or her well-being, taking into account the rights and duties of his or her parents, legal guardians, or other individuals legally responsible for him or her, and, to this end, shall take all appropriate legislative and administrative measures.

3. States Parties shall ensure that the institutions, services and facilities responsible for the care or protection of children shall conform with the standards established by competent authorities, particularly in the areas of safety, health, in the number and suitability of their staff, as well as competent supervision.

Article 4

States Parties shall undertake all appropriate legislative, administrative, and other measures for the implementation of the rights recognized in the present Convention. With regard to economic, social and cultural rights, States Parties shall undertake such measures to the maximum extent of their available resources and, where needed, within the framework of international co-operation.

Article 5

States Parties shall respect the responsibilities, rights and duties of parents or, where applicable, the members of the extended family or community as provided for by local custom, legal guardians or other persons legally responsible for the child, to provide, in a manner consistent with the evolving capacities of the child, appropriate direction and guidance in the exercise by the child of the rights recognized in the present Convention.

Article 6

1. States Parties recognize that every child has the inherent right to life.

2. States Parties shall ensure to the maximum extent possible the survival and development of the child.

Article 7

1. The child shall be registered immediately after birth and shall have the right from birth to a name, the right to acquire a nationality and. as far as possible, the right to know and be cared for by his or her parents.

2. States Parties shall ensure the implementation of these rights in accordance with their national law and their obligations under the relevant international instruments in this field, in particular where the child would otherwise be stateless.

Article 8

1. States Parties undertake to respect the right of the child to preserve his or her identity, including nationality, name and family relations as recognized by law without unlawful interference.

2. Where a child is illegally deprived of some or all of the elements of his or her identity, States Parties shall provide appropriate assistance and protection, with a view to re-establishing speedily his or her identity.

Article 9

1. States Parties shall ensure that a child shall not be separated from his or her parents against their will, except when competent authorities subject to judicial review determine, in accordance with applicable law and procedures, that such separation is necessary for the best interests of the child. Such determination may be necessary in a particular case such as one involving abuse or neglect of the child by the parents, or one where the parents are living separately and a decision must be made as to the child's place of residence.

2. In any proceedings pursuant to paragraph 1 of the present article, all interested parties shall be given an opportunity to participate in the proceedings and make their views known.

3. States Parties shall respect the right of the child who is separated from one or both parents to maintain personal relations and direct contact with both parents on a regular basis, except if it is contrary to the child's best interests.

4. Where such separation results from any action initiated by a State Party, such as the detention, imprisonment, exile, deportation or death (including death arising from any cause while the person is in the custody of the State) of one or both parents or of the child, that State Party shall, upon request, provide the parents, the child or, if appropriate, another member of the family with the essential information concerning the whereabouts of the absent member(s) of the family unless the provision of the information would be detrimental to the well-being of the child. States Parties shall further ensure that the submission of such a request shall of itself entail no adverse consequences for the person(s) concerned.

Article 10

1. In accordance with the obligation of States Parties under article 9, paragraph 1, applications by a child or his or her parents to enter or leave a State Party for the purpose of family reunification shall be dealt with by States Parties in a positive, humane and expeditious manner. States Parties shall further ensure that the submission of such a request shall entail no

adverse consequences for the applicants and for the members of their family.

2. A child whose parents reside in different States shall have the right to maintain on a regular basis, save in exceptional circumstances personal relations and direct contacts with both parents. Towards that end and in accordance with the obligation of States Parties under article 9, paragraph 1, States Parties shall respect the right of the child and his or her parents to leave any country, including their own, and to enter their own country. The right to leave any country shall be subject only to such restrictions as are prescribed by law and which are necessary to protect the national security, public order (ordre public), public health or morals or the rights and freedoms of others and are consistent with the other rights recognized in the present Convention.

Article 11

1. States Parties shall take measures to combat the illicit transfer and non-return of children abroad.

2. To this end, States Parties shall promote the conclusion of bilateral or multilateral agreements or accession to existing agreements.

Article 12

1. States Parties shall assure to the child who is capable of forming his or her own views the right to express those views freely in all matters affecting the child, the views of the child being given due weight in accordance with the age and maturity of the child.

2. For this purpose, the child shall in particular be provided the opportunity to be heard in any judicial and administrative proceedings affecting the child, either directly, or through a representative or an appropriate body, in a manner consistent with the procedural rules of national law.

Article 13

1. The child shall have the right to freedom of expression; this right shall include freedom to seek, receive and impart information and ideas of all kinds, regardless of frontiers, either orally, in writing or in print, in the form of art, or through any other media of the child's choice.

2. The exercise of this right may be subject to certain restrictions, but these shall only be such as are provided by law and are necessary:

    (a) For respect of the rights or reputations of others; or

    (b) For the protection of national security or of public order (ordre public), or of public health or morals.

Article 14

1. States Parties shall respect the right of the child to freedom of thought, conscience and religion.

2. States Parties shall respect the rights and duties of the parents and, when applicable, legal guardians, to provide direction to the child in the exercise of his or her right in a manner consistent with the evolving capacities of the child.

3. Freedom to manifest one's religion or beliefs may be subject only to such limitations as are prescribed by law and are necessary to protect public safety, order, health or morals, or the fundamental rights and freedoms of others.

Article 15

1. States Parties recognize the rights of the child to freedom of association and to freedom of peaceful assembly.

2. No restrictions may be placed on the exercise of these rights other than those imposed in conformity with the law and which are necessary in a democratic society in the interests of national security or public safety, public order (ordre public), the protection of public health or morals or the protection of the rights and freedoms of others.

Article 16

1. No child shall be subjected to arbitrary or unlawful interference with his or her privacy, family, home or correspondence, nor to unlawful attacks on his or her honour and reputation.

2. The child has the right to the protection of the law against such interference or attacks.

Article 17

States Parties recognize the important function performed by the mass media and shall ensure that the child has access to information and material from a diversity of national and international sources, especially those aimed at the promotion of his or her social, spiritual and moral well-being and physical and mental health. To this end, States Parties shall:

(a) Encourage the mass media to disseminate information and material of social and cultural benefit to the child and in accordance with the spirit of article 29;

(b) Encourage international co-operation in the production, exchange and dissemination of such information and material from a diversity of cultural, national and international sources;

(c) Encourage the production and dissemination of children's books;

(d) Encourage the mass media to have particular regard to the linguistic needs of the child who belongs to a minority group or who is indigenous;

(e) Encourage the development of appropriate guidelines for the protection of the child from information and material injurious to his or her well-being, bearing in mind the provisions of articles 13 and 18.

Article 18

1. States Parties shall use their best efforts to ensure recognition of the principle that both parents have common responsibilities for the upbringing and development of the child. Parents or, as the case may be, legal guardians, have the primary responsibility for the upbringing and development of the child. The best interests of the child will be their basic concern.

2. For the purpose of guaranteeing and promoting the rights set forth in the present Convention, States Parties shall render appropriate assistance to parents and legal guardians in the performance of their child-rearing responsibilities and shall ensure the development of institutions, facilities and services for the care of children.

3. States Parties shall take all appropriate measures to ensure that children of working parents have the right to benefit from child-care services and facilities for which they are eligible.

Article 19

1. States Parties shall take all appropriate legislative, administrative, social and educational measures to protect the child from all forms of physical or mental violence, injury or abuse, neglect or negligent treatment, maltreatment or exploitation, including sexual abuse, while in the care of parent(s), legal guardian(s) or any other person who has the care of the child.

2. Such protective measures should, as appropriate, include effective procedures for the establishment of social programmes to provide necessary support for the child and for those who have the care of the child, as well as for other forms of prevention and for identification, reporting, referral, investigation, treatment and follow-up of instances of

child maltreatment described heretofore, and, as appropriate, for judicial involvement.

Article 20

1. A child temporarily or permanently deprived of his or her family environment, or in whose own best interests cannot be allowed to remain in that environment, shall be entitled to special protection and assistance provided by the State.

2. States Parties shall in accordance with their national laws ensure alternative care for such a child.

3. Such care could include, inter alia, foster placement, kafalah of Islamic law, adoption or if necessary placement in suitable institutions for the care of children. When considering solutions, due regard shall be paid to the desirability of continuity in a child's upbringing and to the child's ethnic, religious, cultural and linguistic background.

Article 21

States Parties that recognize and/or permit the system of adoption shall ensure that the best interests of the child shall be the paramount consideration and they shall:

(a) Ensure that the adoption of a child is authorized only by competent authorities who determine, in accordance with applicable law and procedures and on the basis of all pertinent and reliable information, that the adoption is permissible in view of the child's status concerning parents, relatives and legal guardians and that, if required, the persons concerned have given their informed consent to the adoption on the basis of such counselling as may be necessary;

(b) Recognize that inter-country adoption may be considered as an alternative means of child's care, if the child cannot be placed in a foster or an adoptive family or cannot in any suitable manner be cared for in the child's country of origin;

(c) Ensure that the child concerned by inter-country adoption enjoys safeguards and standards equivalent to those existing in the case of national adoption;

(d) Take all appropriate measures to ensure that, in inter-country adoption, the placement does not result in improper financial gain for those involved in it;

(e) Promote, where appropriate, the objectives of the present article by concluding bilateral or multilateral arrangements or agreements, and endeavour, within this framework, to ensure that the placement of the child in another country is carried out by competent authorities or organs.

Article 22

1. States Parties shall take appropriate measures to ensure that a child who is seeking refugee status or who is considered a refugee in accordance with applicable international or domestic law and procedures shall, whether unaccompanied or accompanied by his or her parents or by any other person, receive appropriate protection and humanitarian assistance in the enjoyment of applicable rights set forth in the present Convention and in other international human rights or humanitarian instruments to which the said States are Parties.

2. For this purpose, States Parties shall provide, as they consider appropriate, co-operation in any efforts by the United Nations and other competent intergovernmental organizations or non-governmental organizations co-operating with the United Nations to protect and assist such a child and to trace the parents or other members of the family of any refugee child in order to obtain information necessary for reunification with his or her family. In cases where no parents or other members of the family can be found, the child shall be accorded the same protection as any other child permanently or temporarily deprived of his or her family environment for any reason , as set forth in the present Convention.

Article 23

1. States Parties recognize that a mentally or physically disabled child should enjoy a full and decent life, in conditions which ensure dignity, promote self-reliance and facilitate the child's active participation in the community.

2. States Parties recognize the right of the disabled child to special care and shall encourage and ensure the extension, subject to available resources, to the eligible child and those responsible for his or her care, of assistance for which application is made and which is appropriate to the child's condition and to the circumstances of the parents or others caring for the child.

3. Recognizing the special needs of a disabled child, assistance extended in accordance with paragraph 2 of the present article shall be provided free of charge, whenever possible, taking into account the financial resources of the parents or others caring for the child, and shall be designed to ensure that the disabled child has effective access to and receives education, training, health care services, rehabilitation services, preparation for employment and recreation opportunities in a manner conducive to the child's achieving the fullest possible social integration

and individual development, including his or her cultural and spiritual development

4. States Parties shall promote, in the spirit of international cooperation, the exchange of appropriate information in the field of preventive health care and of medical, psychological and functional treatment of disabled children, including dissemination of and access to information concerning methods of rehabilitation, education and vocational services, with the aim of enabling States Parties to improve their capabilities and skills and to widen their experience in these areas. In this regard, particular account shall be taken of the needs of developing countries.

Article 24

1. States Parties recognize the right of the child to the enjoyment of the highest attainable standard of health and to facilities for the treatment of illness and rehabilitation of health. States Parties shall strive to ensure that no child is deprived of his or her right of access to such health care services.

2. States Parties shall pursue full implementation of this right and, in particular, shall take appropriate measures:

(a) To diminish infant and child mortality;

(b) To ensure the provision of necessary medical assistance and health care to all children with emphasis on the development of primary health care;

(c) To combat disease and malnutrition, including within the framework of primary health care, through, inter alia, the application of readily available technology and through the provision of adequate nutritious foods and clean drinking-water, taking into consideration the dangers and risks of environmental pollution;

(d) To ensure appropriate pre-natal and post-natal health care for mothers;

(e) To ensure that all segments of society, in particular parents and children, are informed, have access to education and are supported in the use of basic knowledge of child health and nutrition, the advantages of breastfeeding, hygiene and environmental sanitation and the prevention of accidents;

(f) To develop preventive health care, guidance for parents and family planning education and services.

3. States Parties shall take all effective and appropriate measures with a view to abolishing traditional practices prejudicial to the health of children.

4. States Parties undertake to promote and encourage international co-operation with a view to achieving progressively the full realization of the right recognized in the present article. In this regard, particular account shall be taken of the needs of developing countries.

Article 25

States Parties recognize the right of a child who has been placed by the competent authorities for the purposes of care, protection or treatment of his or her physical or mental health, to a periodic review of the treatment provided to the child and all other circumstances relevant to his or her placement.

Article 26

1. States Parties shall recognize for every child the right to benefit from social security, including social insurance, and shall take the necessary measures to achieve the full realization of this right in accordance with their national law.

2. The benefits should, where appropriate, be granted, taking into account the resources and the circumstances of the child and persons having responsibility for the maintenance of the child, as well as any other consideration relevant to an application for benefits made by or on behalf of the child.

Article 27

1. States Parties recognize the right of every child to a standard of living adequate for the child's physical, mental, spiritual, moral and social development.

2. The parent(s) or others responsible for the child have the primary responsibility to secure, within their abilities and financial capacities, the conditions of living necessary for the child's development.

3. States Parties, in accordance with national conditions and within their means, shall take appropriate measures to assist parents and others responsible for the child to implement this right and shall in case of need provide material assistance and support programmes, particularly with regard to nutrition, clothing and housing.

4. States Parties shall take all appropriate measures to secure the recovery of maintenance for the child from the parents or other persons having

financial responsibility for the child, both within the State Party and from abroad. In particular, where the person having financial responsibility for the child lives in a State different from that of the child, States Parties shall promote the accession to international agreements or the conclusion of such agreements, as well as the making of other appropriate arrangements.

Article 28

1. States Parties recognize the right of the child to education, and with a view to achieving this right progressively and on the basis of equal opportunity, they shall, in particular:

   (a) Make primary education compulsory and available free to all;

   (b) Encourage the development of different forms of secondary education, including general and vocational education, make them available and accessible to every child, and take appropriate measures such as the introduction of free education and offering financial assistance in case of need;

   (c) Make higher education accessible to all on the basis of capacity by every appropriate means;

   (d) Make educational and vocational information and guidance available and accessible to all children;

   (e) Take measures to encourage regular attendance at schools and the reduction of drop-out rates.

2. States Parties shall take all appropriate measures to ensure that school discipline is administered in a manner consistent with the child's human dignity and in conformity with the present Convention.

3. States Parties shall promote and encourage international cooperation in matters relating to education, in particular with a view to contributing to the elimination of ignorance and illiteracy throughout the world and facilitating access to scientific and technical knowledge and modern teaching methods. In this regard, particular account shall be taken of the needs of developing countries.

Article 29

1. States Parties agree that the education of the child shall be directed to:

   (a) The development of the child's personality, talents and mental and physical abilities to their fullest potential;

(b) The development of respect for human rights and fundamental freedoms, and for the principles enshrined in the Charter of the United Nations;

(c) The development of respect for the child's parents, his or her own cultural identity, language and values, for the national values of the country in which the child is living, the country from which he or she may originate, and for civilizations different from his or her own;

(d) The preparation of the child for responsible life in a free society, in the spirit of understanding, peace, tolerance, equality of sexes, and friendship among all peoples, ethnic, national and religious groups and persons of indigenous origin;

(e) The development of respect for the natural environment.

2. No part of the present article or article 28 shall be construed so as to interfere with the liberty of individuals and bodies to establish and direct educational institutions, subject always to the observance of the principle set forth in paragraph 1 of the present article and to the requirements that the education given in such institutions shall conform to such minimum standards as may be laid down by the State.

Article 30

In those States in which ethnic, religious or linguistic minorities or persons of indigenous origin exist, a child belonging to such a minority or who is indigenous shall not be denied the right, in community with other members of his or her group, to enjoy his or her own culture, to profess and practise his or her own religion, or to use his or her own language.

Article 31

1. States Parties recognize the right of the child to rest and leisure, to engage in play and recreational activities appropriate to the age of the child and to participate freely in cultural life and the arts.

2. States Parties shall respect and promote the right of the child to participate fully in cultural and artistic life and shall encourage the provision of appropriate and equal opportunities for cultural, artistic, recreational and leisure activity.

Article 32

1. States Parties recognize the right of the child to be protected from economic exploitation and from performing any work that is likely to be

hazardous or to interfere with the child's education, or to be harmful to the child's health or physical, mental, spiritual, moral or social development.

2. States Parties shall take legislative, administrative, social and educational measures to ensure the implementation of the present article. To this end, and having regard to the relevant provisions of other international instruments, States Parties shall in particular:

(a) Provide for a minimum age or minimum ages for admission to employment;

(b) Provide for appropriate regulation of the hours and conditions of employment;

(c) Provide for appropriate penalties or other sanctions to ensure the effective enforcement of the present article.

Article 33

States Parties shall take all appropriate measures, including legislative, administrative, social and educational measures, to protect children from the illicit use of narcotic drugs and psychotropic substances as defined in the relevant international treaties, and to prevent the use of children in the illicit production and trafficking of such substances.

Article 34

States Parties undertake to protect the child from all forms of sexual exploitation and sexual abuse. For these purposes, States Parties shall in particular take all appropriate national, bilateral and multilateral measures to prevent:

(a) The inducement or coercion of a child to engage in any unlawful sexual activity;

(b) The exploitative use of children in prostitution or other unlawful sexual practices;

(c) The exploitative use of children in pornographic performances and materials.

Article 35

States Parties shall take all appropriate national, bilateral and multilateral measures to prevent the abduction of, the sale of or traffic in children for any purpose or in any form.

Article 36

States Parties shall protect the child against all other forms of exploitation prejudicial to any aspects of the child's welfare.

Article 37

States Parties shall ensure that:

(a) No child shall be subjected to torture or other cruel, inhuman or degrading treatment or punishment. Neither capital punishment nor life imprisonment without possibility of release shall be imposed for offences committed by persons below eighteen years of age;

(b) No child shall be deprived of his or her liberty unlawfully or arbitrarily. The arrest, detention or imprisonment of a child shall be in conformity with the law and shall be used only as a measure of last resort and for the shortest appropriate period of time;

(c) Every child deprived of liberty shall be treated with humanity and respect for the inherent dignity of the human person, and in a manner which takes into account the needs of persons of his or her age. In particular, every child deprived of liberty shall be separated from adults unless it is considered in the child's best interest not to do so and shall have the right to maintain contact with his or her family through correspondence and visits, save in exceptional circumstances;

(d) Every child deprived of his or her liberty shall have the right to prompt access to legal and other appropriate assistance, as well as the right to challenge the legality of the deprivation of his or her liberty before a court or other competent, independent and impartial authority, and to a prompt decision on any such action.

Article 38

1. States Parties undertake to respect and to ensure respect for rules of international humanitarian law applicable to them in armed conflicts which are relevant to the child.

2. States Parties shall take all feasible measures to ensure that persons who have not attained the age of fifteen years do not take a direct part in hostilities.

3. States Parties shall refrain from recruiting any person who has not attained the age of fifteen years into their armed forces. In recruiting among those persons who have attained the age of fifteen years but who have not attained the age of eighteen years, States Parties shall endeavour to give priority to those who are oldest.

4. In accordance with their obligations under international humanitarian law to protect the civilian population in armed conflicts, States Parties shall take all feasible measures to ensure protection and care of children who are affected by an armed conflict.

Article 39

States Parties shall take all appropriate measures to promote physical and psychological recovery and social reintegration of a child victim of: any form of neglect, exploitation, or abuse; torture or any other form of cruel, inhuman or degrading treatment or punishment; or armed conflicts. Such recovery and reintegration shall take place in an environment which fosters the health, self-respect and dignity of the child.

Article 40

1. States Parties recognize the right of every child alleged as, accused of, or recognized as having infringed the penal law to be treated in a manner consistent with the promotion of the child's sense of dignity and worth, which reinforces the child's respect for the human rights and fundamental freedoms of others and which takes into account the child's age and the desirability of promoting the child's reintegration and the child's assuming a constructive role in society.

2. To this end, and having regard to the relevant provisions of international instruments, States Parties shall, in particular, ensure that:

    (a) No child shall be alleged as, be accused of, or recognized as having infringed the penal law by reason of acts or omissions that were not prohibited by national or international law at the time they were committed;

    (b) Every child alleged as or accused of having infringed the penal law has at least the following guarantees:

        (i) To be presumed innocent until proven guilty according to law;

        (ii) To be informed promptly and directly of the charges against him or her, and, if appropriate, through his or her parents or legal guardians, and to have legal or other appropriate assistance in the preparation and presentation of his or her defence;

        (iii) To have the matter determined without delay by a competent, independent and impartial authority or judicial body in a fair hearing according to law, in the presence of legal or other appropriate assistance and, unless it is considered not to be in the best interest of the child, in particular, taking into account his or her age or situation, his or her parents or legal guardians;

(iv) Not to be compelled to give testimony or to confess guilt; to examine or have examined adverse witnesses and to obtain the participation and examination of witnesses on his or her behalf under conditions of equality;

(v) If considered to have infringed the penal law, to have this decision and any measures imposed in consequence thereof reviewed by a higher competent, independent and impartial authority or judicial body according to law;

(vi) To have the free assistance of an interpreter if the child cannot understand or speak the language used;

(vii) To have his or her privacy fully respected at all stages of the proceedings.

3. States Parties shall seek to promote the establishment of laws, procedures, authorities and institutions specifically applicable to children alleged as, accused of, or recognized as having infringed the penal law, and, in particular:

(a) The establishment of a minimum age below which children shall be presumed not to have the capacity to infringe the penal law;

(b) Whenever appropriate and desirable, measures for dealing with such children without resorting to judicial proceedings, providing that human rights and legal safeguards are fully respected.

4. A variety of dispositions, such as care, guidance and supervision orders; counselling; probation; foster care; education and vocational training programmes and other alternatives to institutional care shall be available to ensure that children are dealt with in a manner appropriate to their well-being and proportionate both to their circumstances and the offence.

Article 41

Nothing in the present Convention shall affect any provisions which are more conducive to the realization of the rights of the child and which may be contained in:

(a) The law of a State party; or

(b) International law in force for that State.

Part II

Article 42

States Parties undertake to make the principles and provisions of the Convention widely known, by appropriate and active means, to adults and children alike.

8.   Principles Relating to the Status of National Institutions — "Paris Principles"

Adopted by General Assembly resolution 48/134 of 10 December 1993.

Competence and responsibilities

1. A national institution shall be vested with competence to promote and protect human rights.

2. A national institution shall be given as broad a mandate as possible, which shall be clearly set forth in a constitutional or legislative text, specifying its composition and its sphere of competence.

3. A national institution shall, inter alia, have the following responsibilities:

(a) To submit to the Government, Parliament and any other competent body, on an advisory basis either at the request of the authorities concerned or through the exercise of its power to hear a matter without higher referral, opinions, recommendations, proposals and reports on any matters concerning the promotion and protection of human rights; the national institution may decide to publicize them; these opinions, recommendations, proposals and reports, as well as any prerogative of the national institution, shall relate to the following areas:

(i)   Any legislative or administrative provisions, as well as provisions relating to judicial organizations, intended to preserve and extend the protection of human rights; in that connection, the national institution shall examine the legislation and administrative provisions in force, as well as bills and proposals, and shall make such recommendations as it deems appropriate in order to ensure that these provisions conform to the fundamental principles of human rights; it shall, if necessary, recommend the adoption of new legislation, the amendment of legislation in force and the adoption or amendment of administrative measures;

    (ii)   Any situation of violation of human rights which it decides to take up;

    (iii)   The preparation of reports on the national situation with regard to human rights in general, and on more specific matters;

    (iv)   Drawing the attention of the Government to situations in any part of the country where human rights are violated and making proposals to it for initiatives to put an end to such situations and, where necessary, expressing an opinion on the positions and reactions of the Government;

(b) To promote and ensure the harmonization of national legislation regulations and practices with the international human rights instruments to which the State is a party, and their effective implementation;

(c) To encourage ratification of the above-mentioned instruments or accession to those instruments, and to ensure their implementation;

(d) To contribute to the reports which States are required to submit to United Nations bodies and committees, and to regional institutions, pursuant to their treaty obligations and, where necessary, to express an opinion on the subject, with due respect for their independence;

(e) To cooperate with the United Nations and any other organization in the United Nations system, the regional institutions and the national institutions of other countries that are competent in the areas of the promotion and protection of human rights;

(f) To assist in the formulation of programmes for the teaching of, and research into, human rights and to take part in their execution in schools, universities and professional circles;

(g) To publicize human rights and efforts to combat all forms of discrimination, in particular racial discrimination, by increasing public awareness, especially through information and education and by making use of all press organs.

Composition and guarantees of independence and pluralism

1. The composition of the national institution and the appointment of its members, whether by means of an election or otherwise, shall be established in accordance with a procedure which affords all necessary guarantees to ensure the pluralist representation of the social forces (of civilian society) involved in the promotion and protection of human

rights, particularly by powers which will enable effective cooperation to be established with, or through the presence of, representatives of:

(a) Non-governmental organizations responsible for human rights and efforts to combat racial discrimination, trade unions, concerned social and professional organizations, for example, associations of lawyers, doctors, journalists and eminent scientists;

(b) Trends in philosophical or religious thought;

(c) Universities and qualified experts;

(d) Parliament;

(e) Government departments (if these are included, their representatives should participate in the deliberations only in an advisory capacity).

2. The national institution shall have an infrastructure which is suited to the smooth conduct of its activities, in particular adequate funding. The purpose of this funding should be to enable it to have its own staff and premises, in order to be independent of the Government and not be subject to financial control which might affect its independence.

3. In order to ensure a stable mandate for the members of the national institution, without which there can be no real independence, their appointment shall be effected by an official act which shall establish the specific duration of the mandate. This mandate may be renewable, provided that the pluralism of the institution's membership is ensured.

Methods of operation

Within the framework of its operation, the national institution shall:

(a) Freely consider any questions falling within its competence, whether they are submitted by the Government or taken up by it without referral to a higher authority, on the proposal of its members or of any petitioner;

(b) Hear any person and obtain any information and any documents necessary for assessing situations falling within its competence;

(c) Address public opinion directly or through any press organ, particularly in order to publicize its opinions and recommendations;

(d) Meet on a regular basis and whenever necessary in the presence of all its members after they have been duly convened;

(e) Establish working groups from among its members as necessary, and set up local or regional sections to assist it in discharging its functions;

(f) Maintain consultation with the other bodies, whether jurisdictional or otherwise, responsible for the promotion and protection of human rights (in particular ombudsmen, mediators and similar institutions);

(g) In view of the fundamental role played by the non-governmental organizations in expanding the work of the national institutions, develop relations with the non-governmental organizations devoted to promoting and protecting human rights, to economic and social development, to combatting racism, to protecting particularly vulnerable groups (especially children, migrant workers, refugees, physically and mentally disabled persons) or to specialized areas.

Additional principles concerning the status of commissions with quasi-jurisdictional competence

A national institution may be authorized to hear and consider complaints and petitions concerning individual situations. Cases may be brought before it by individuals, their representatives, third parties, non-governmental organizations, associations of trade unions or any other representative organizations. In such circumstances, and without prejudice to the principles stated above concerning the other powers of the commissions, the functions entrusted to them may be based on the following principles:

(a) Seeking an amicable settlement through conciliation or, within the limits prescribed by the law, through binding decisions or, where necessary, on the basis of confidentiality;

(b) Informing the party who filed the petition of his rights, in particular the remedies available to him, and promoting his access to them;

(c) Hearing any complaints or petitions or transmitting them to any other competent authority within the limits prescribed by the law;

(d) Making recommendations to the competent authorities, especially by proposing amendments or reforms of the laws, regulations and administrative practices, especially if they have created the difficulties encountered by the persons filing the petitions in order to assert their rights.

9.   Vienna Declaration and Programme of Action

World Conference on Human Rights, 14-25 June 1993, Vienna, Austria, U.N. Doc. A/CONF.157/24 (Part I) at 20 (1993).

I

1. The World Conference on Human Rights reaffirms the solemn commitment of all States to fulfil their obligations to promote universal respect for, and observance and protection of, all human rights and fundamental freedoms for all in accordance with the *Charter* of the United Nations, other instruments relating to human rights, and international law. The universal nature of these rights and freedoms is beyond question.

In this framework, enhancement of international cooperation in the field of human rights is essential for the full achievement of the purposes of the United Nations.

Human rights and fundamental freedoms are the birthright of all human beings; their protection and promotion is the first responsibility of Governments.

...

5. All human rights are universal, indivisible and interdependent and interrelated. The international community must treat human rights globally in a fair and equal manner, on the same footing, and with the same emphasis. While the significance of national and regional particularities and various historical, cultural and religious backgrounds must be borne in mind, it is the duty of States, regardless of their political, economic and cultural systems, to promote and protect all human rights and fundamental freedoms.

II.   REGIONAL

1.   American Declaration of the Rights and Duties of Man

O.A.S. Res. XXX, adopted by the Ninth International Conference of American States (1948), reprinted in Basic Documents Pertaining to Human Rights in the Inter-American System, OEA/Ser.L.V/II.82 doc.6 rev.1 at 17 (1992).

WHEREAS:

The American peoples have acknowledged the dignity of the individual, and their national constitutions recognize that juridical and political institutions, which regulate life in human society, have as their principal aim the protection of the essential rights of man and the creation of circumstances that will permit him to achieve spiritual and material progress and attain happiness;

The American States have on repeated occasions recognized that the essential rights of man are not derived from the fact that he is a national of a certain state, but are based upon attributes of his human personality;

The international protection of the rights of man should be the principal guide of an evolving American law;

The affirmation of essential human rights by the American States together with the guarantees given by the internal regimes of the states establish the initial system of protection considered by the American States as being suited to the present social and juridical conditions, not without a recognition on their part that they should increasingly strengthen that system in the international field as conditions become more favorable,

The Ninth International Conference of American States

AGREES:

To adopt the following

American Declaration of the Rights and Duties of Man

Preamble

All men are born free and equal, in dignity and in rights, and, being endowed by nature with reason and conscience, they should conduct themselves as brothers one to another.

The fulfillment of duty by each individual is a prerequisite to the rights of all. Rights and duties are interrelated in every social and political activity of man. While rights exalt individual liberty, duties express the dignity of that liberty.

Duties of a juridical nature presuppose others of a moral nature which support them in principle and constitute their basis.

Inasmuch as spiritual development is the supreme end of human existence and the highest expression thereof, it is the duty of man to serve that end with all his strength and resources.

Since culture is the highest social and historical expression of that spiritual development, it is the duty of man to preserve, practice and foster culture by every means within his power.

And, since moral conduct constitutes the noblest flowering of culture, it is the duty of every man always to hold it in high respect.

Chapter One

Rights

Article I

Every human being has the right to life, liberty and the security of his person.

Article II

All persons are equal before the law and have the rights and duties established in this Declaration, without distinction as to race, sex, language, creed or any other factor.

Article III

Every person has the right freely to profess a religious faith, and to manifest and practice it both in public and in private.

Article IV

Every person has the right to freedom of investigation, of opinion, and of the expression and dissemination of ideas, by any medium whatsoever.

Article V

Every person has the right to the protection of the law against abusive attacks upon his honor, his reputation, and his private and family life.

Article VI

Every person has the right to establish a family, the basic element of society, and to receive protection therefor.

Article VII

All women, during pregnancy and the nursing period, and all children have the right to special protection, care and aid.

Article VIII

Every person has the right to fix his residence within the territory of the state of which he is a national, to move about freely within such territory, and not to leave it except by his own will.

Article IX

Every person has the right to the inviolability of his home.

Article X

Every person has the right to the inviolability and transmission of his correspondence.

Article XI

Every person has the right to the preservation of his health through sanitary and social measures relating to food, clothing, housing and medical care, to the extent permitted by public and community resources.

Article XII

Every person has the right to an education, which should be based on the principles of liberty, morality and human solidarity.

Likewise every person has the right to an education that will prepare him to attain a decent life, to raise his standard of living, and to be a useful member of society. The right to an education includes the right to equality of opportunity in every case, in accordance with natural talents, merit and the desire to utilize the resources that the state or the community is in a position to provide. Every person has the right to receive, free, at least a primary education.

Article XIII

Every person has the right to take part in the cultural life of the community, to enjoy the arts, and to participate in the benefits that result from intellectual progress, especially scientific discoveries.

He likewise has the right to the protection of his moral and material interests as regards his inventions or any literary, scientific or artistic works of which he is the author.

Article XIV

Every person has the right to work, under proper conditions, and to follow his vocation freely, in sofar as existing conditions of employment permit.

Every person who works has the right to receive such remuneration as will, in proportion to his capacity and skill, assure him a standard of living suitable for himself and for his family.

Article XV

Every person has the right to leisure time, to wholesome recreation, and to the opportunity for advantageous use of his free time to his spiritual, cultural and physical benefit.

Article XVI

Every person has the right to social security which will protect him from the consequences of unemployment, old age, and any disabilities arising from causes beyond his control that make it physically or mentally impossible for him to earn a living.

Article XVII

Every person has the right to be recognized everywhere as a person having rights and obligations, and to enjoy the basic civil rights.

Article XVIII

Every person may resort to the courts to ensure respect for his legal rights. There should likewise be available to him a simple, brief procedure whereby the courts will protect him from acts of authority that, to his prejudice, violate any fundamental constitutional rights.

Article XIX

Every person has the right to the nationality to which he is entitled by law and to change it, if he so wishes, for the nationality of any other country that is willing to grant it to him.

Article XX

Every person having legal capacity is entitled to participate in the government of his country, directly or through his representatives, and to take part in popular elections, which shall be by secret ballot, and shall be honest, periodic and free.

Article XXI

Every person has the right to assemble peaceably with others in a formal public meeting or an informal gathering, in connection with matters of common interest of any nature.

Article XXII

Every person has the right to associate with others to promote, exercise and protect his legitimate interests of a political, economic, religious, social, cultural, professional, labor union or other nature.

Article XXIII

Every person has a right to own such private property as meets the essential needs of decent living and helps to maintain the dignity of the individual and of the home.

Article XXIV

Every person has the right to submit respectful petitions to any competent authority, for reasons of either general or private interest, and the right to obtain a prompt decision thereon.

Article XXV

No person may be deprived of his liberty except in the cases and according to the procedures established by pre-existing law.

No person may be deprived of liberty for nonfulfillment of obligations of a purely civil character.

Every individual who has been deprived of his liberty has the right to have the legality of his detention ascertained without delay by a court, and the right to be tried without undue delay or, otherwise, to be released. He also has the right to humane treatment during the time he is in custody.

Article XXVI

Every accused person is presumed to be innocent until proved guilty.

Every person accused of an offense has the right to be given an impartial and public hearing, and to be tried by courts previously established in accordance with pre-existing laws, and not to receive cruel, infamous or unusual punishment.

Article XXVII

Every person has the right, in case of pursuit not resulting from ordinary crimes, to seek and receive asylum in foreign territory, in accordance with the laws of each country and with international agreements.

Article XXVIII

The rights of man are limited by the rights of others, by the security of all, and by the just demands of the general welfare and the advancement of democracy.

Chapter Two

Duties

Article XXIX

It is the duty of the individual so to conduct himself in relation to others that each and every one may fully form and develop his personality.

Article XXX

It is the duty of every person to aid, support, educate and protect his minor children, and it is the duty of children to honor their parents always and to aid, support and protect them when they need it.

Article XXXI

It is the duty of every person to acquire at least an elementary education.

Article XXXII

It is the duty of every person to vote in the popular elections of the country of which he is a national, when he is legally capable of doing so.

Article XXXIII

It is the duty of every person to obey the law and other legitimate commands of the authorities of his country and those of the country in which he may be.

Article XXXIV

It is the duty of every able-bodied person to render whatever civil and military service his country may require for its defense and preservation, and, in case of public disaster, to render such services as may be in his power.

It is likewise his duty to hold any public office to which he may be elected by popular vote in the state of which he is a national.

Article XXXV

It is the duty of every person to cooperate with the state and the community with respect to social security and welfare, in accordance with his ability and with existing circumstances.

Article XXXVI

It is the duty of every person to pay the taxes established by law for the support of public services.

Article XXXVII

It is the duty of every person to work, as far as his capacity and possibilities permit, in order to obtain the means of livelihood or to benefit his community.

Article XXXVIII

It is the duty of every person to refrain from taking part in political activities that, according to law, are reserved exclusively to the citizens of the state in which he is an alien.

2.   American Convention on Human Rights

O.A.S. Treaty Series No. 36, 1144 U.N.T.S. 123 entered into force July 18, 1978, reprinted in Basic Documents Pertaining to Human Rights in the Inter-American System, OEA/Ser.L.V/II.82 doc.6 rev.1 at 25 (1992).

(NOTE: Canada is not a signatory to this Convention.)

Preamble

The American states signatory to the present Convention,

Reaffirming their intention to consolidate in this hemisphere, within the framework of democratic institutions, a system of personal liberty and social justice based on respect for the essential rights of man;

Recognizing that the essential rights of man are not derived from one's being a national of a certain state, but are based upon attributes of the human personality, and that they therefore justify international protection in the form of a convention reinforcing or complementing the protection provided by the domestic law of the American states;

Considering that these principles have been set forth in the Charter of the Organization of American States, in the American Declaration of the Rights and Duties of Man, and in the Universal Declaration of Human Rights, and that they have been reaffirmed and refined in other international instruments, worldwide as well as regional in scope;

Reiterating that, in accordance with the Universal Declaration of Human Rights, the ideal of free men enjoying freedom from fear and want can be achieved only if conditions are created whereby everyone may enjoy his economic, social, and cultural rights, as well as his civil and political rights; and

Considering that the Third Special Inter-American Conference (Buenos Aires, 1967) approved the incorporation into the Charter of the Organization itself of broader standards with respect to economic, social, and educational rights and resolved that an inter-American convention on human rights should determine the structure, competence, and procedure of the organs responsible for these matters,

Have agreed upon the following:

PART I - STATE OBLIGATIONS AND RIGHTS PROTECTED

Chapter I — General Obligations

Article 1. Obligation to Respect Rights

1. The States Parties to this Convention undertake to respect the rights and freedoms recognized herein and to ensure to all persons subject to their jurisdiction the free and full exercise of those rights and freedoms, without any discrimination for reasons of race, color, sex, language, religion, political or other opinion, national or social origin, economic status, birth, or any other social condition.

2. For the purposes of this Convention, "person" means every human being.

Article 2. Domestic Legal Effects

Where the exercise of any of the rights or freedoms referred to in Article 1 is not already ensured by legislative or other provisions, the States Parties undertake to adopt, in accordance with their constitutional processes and the provisions of this Convention, such legislative or other measures as may be necessary to give effect to those rights or freedoms.

Chapter II — Civil and Political Rights

Article 3. Right to Juridical Personality

Every person has the right to recognition as a person before the law.

Article 4. Right to Life

1. Every person has the right to have his life respected. This right shall be protected by law and, in general, from the moment of conception. No one shall be arbitrarily deprived of his life.

2. In countries that have not abolished the death penalty, it may be imposed only for the most serious crimes and pursuant to a final judgment rendered by a competent court and in accordance with a law establishing such punishment, enacted prior to the commission of the crime. The application of such punishment shall not be extended to crimes to which it does not presently apply.

3. The death penalty shall not be reestablished in states that have abolished it.

4. In no case shall capital punishment be inflicted for political offenses or related common crimes.

5. Capital punishment shall not be imposed upon persons who, at the time the crime was committed, were under 18 years of age or over 70 years of age; nor shall it be applied to pregnant women.

6. Every person condemned to death shall have the right to apply for amnesty, pardon, or commutation of sentence, which may be granted in all cases. Capital punishment shall not be imposed while such a petition is pending decision by the competent authority.

Article 5. Right to Humane Treatment

1. Every person has the right to have his physical, mental, and moral integrity respected.

2. No one shall be subjected to torture or to cruel, inhuman, or degrading punishment or treatment. All persons deprived of their liberty shall be treated with respect for the inherent dignity of the human person.

3. Punishment shall not be extended to any person other than the criminal.

4. Accused persons shall, save in exceptional circumstances, be segregated from convicted persons, and shall be subject to separate treatment appropriate to their status as unconvicted persons.

5. Minors while subject to criminal proceedings shall be separated from adults and brought before specialized tribunals, as speedily as possible, so that they may be treated in accordance with their status as minors.

6. Punishments consisting of deprivation of liberty shall have as an essential aim the reform and social readaptation of the prisoners.

Article 6. Freedom from Slavery

1. No one shall be subject to slavery or to involuntary servitude, which are prohibited in all their forms, as are the slave trade and traffic in women.

2. No one shall be required to perform forced or compulsory labor. This provision shall not be interpreted to mean that, in those countries in which the penalty established for certain crimes is deprivation of liberty at forced labor, the carrying out of such a sentence imposed by a competent court is prohibited. Forced labor shall not adversely affect the dignity or the physical or intellectual capacity of the prisoner.

3. For the purposes of this article, the following do not constitute forced or compulsory labor:

    a.   work or service normally required of a person imprisoned in execution of a sentence or formal decision passed by the competent judicial authority. Such work or service shall be carried out under the supervision and control of public authorities, and any persons performing such work or service shall not be placed at the disposal of any private party, company, or juridical person;

    b.   military service and, in countries in which conscientious objectors are recognized, national service that the law may provide for in lieu of military service;

    c.   service exacted in time of danger or calamity that threatens the existence or the well-being of the community; or

    d.   work or service that forms part of normal civic obligations.

Article 7. Right to Personal Liberty

1. Every person has the right to personal liberty and security.

2. No one shall be deprived of his physical liberty except for the reasons and under the conditions established beforehand by the constitution of the State Party concerned or by a law established pursuant thereto.

3. No one shall be subject to arbitrary arrest or imprisonment.

4. Anyone who is detained shall be informed of the reasons for his detention and shall be promptly notified of the charge or charges against him.

5. Any person detained shall be brought promptly before a judge or other officer authorized by law to exercise judicial power and shall be entitled to trial within a reasonable time or to be released without prejudice to the continuation of the proceedings. His release may be subject to guarantees to assure his appearance for trial.

6. Anyone who is deprived of his liberty shall be entitled to recourse to a competent court, in order that the court may decide without delay on the lawfulness of his arrest or detention and order his release if the arrest or detention is unlawful. In States Parties whose laws provide that anyone who believes himself to be threatened with deprivation of his liberty is entitled to recourse to a competent court in order that it may decide on the lawfulness of such threat, this remedy may not be restricted or abolished. The interested party or another person in his behalf is entitled to seek these remedies.

7. No one shall be detained for debt. This principle shall not limit the orders of a competent judicial authority issued for nonfulfillment of duties of support.

Article 8. Right to a Fair Trial

1. Every person has the right to a hearing, with due guarantees and within a reasonable time, by a competent, independent, and impartial tribunal, previously established by law, in the substantiation of any accusation of a criminal nature made against him or for the determination of his rights and obligations of a civil, labor, fiscal, or any other nature.

2. Every person accused of a criminal offense has the right to be presumed innocent so long as his guilt has not been proven according to law. During the proceedings, every person is entitled, with full equality, to the following minimum guarantees:

   a. the right of the accused to be assisted without charge by a transla-tor or interpreter, if he does not understand or does not speak the language of the tribunal or court;

   b. prior notification in detail to the accused of the charges against him;

   c. adequate time and means for the preparation of his defense;

   d. the right of the accused to defend himself personally or to be as-sisted by legal counsel of his own choosing, and to communicate freely and privately with his counsel;

   e. the inalienable right to be assisted by counsel provided by the state, paid or not as the domestic law provides, if the accused does not defend himself personally or engage his own counsel within the time period established by law;

   f. the right of the defense to examine witnesses present in the court and to obtain the appearance, as witnesses, of experts or other per-sons who may throw light on the facts;

g. the right not to be compelled to be a witness against himself or to plead guilty; and

h. the right to appeal the judgment to a higher court.

3. A confession of guilt by the accused shall be valid only if it is made without coercion of any kind.

4. An accused person acquitted by a nonappealable judgment shall not be subjected to a new trial for the same cause.

5. Criminal proceedings shall be public, except insofar as may be necessary to protect the interests of justice.

Article 9. Freedom from Ex Post Facto Laws

No one shall be convicted of any act or omission that did not constitute a criminal offense, under the applicable law, at the time it was committed. A heavier penalty shall not be imposed than the one that was applicable at the time the criminal offense was committed. If subsequent to the commission of the offense the law provides for the imposition of a lighter punishment, the guilty person shall benefit therefrom.

Article 10. Right to Compensation

Every person has the right to be compensated in accordance with the law in the event he has been sentenced by a final judgment through a miscarriage of justice.

Article 11. Right to Privacy

1. Everyone has the right to have his honor respected and his dignity recognized.

2. No one may be the object of arbitrary or abusive interference with his private life, his family, his home, or his correspondence, or of unlawful attacks on his honor or reputation.

3. Everyone has the right to the protection of the law against such interference or attacks.

Article 12. Freedom of Conscience and Religion

1. Everyone has the right to freedom of conscience and of religion. This right includes freedom to maintain or to change one's religion or beliefs, and freedom to profess or disseminate one's religion or beliefs, either individually or together with others, in public or in private.

2. No one shall be subject to restrictions that might impair his freedom to maintain or to change his religion or beliefs.

3. Freedom to manifest one's religion and beliefs may be subject only to the limitations prescribed by law that are necessary to protect public safety, order, health, or morals, or the rights or freedoms of others.

4. Parents or guardians, as the case may be, have the right to provide for the religious and moral education of their children or wards that is in accord with their own convictions.

Article 13. Freedom of Thought and Expression

1. Everyone has the right to freedom of thought and expression. This right includes freedom to seek, receive, and impart information and ideas of all kinds, regardless of frontiers, either orally, in writing, in print, in the form of art, or through any other medium of one's choice.

2. The exercise of the right provided for in the foregoing paragraph shall not be subject to prior censorship but shall be subject to subsequent imposition of liability, which shall be expressly established by law to the extent necessary to ensure:

    a.   respect for the rights or reputations of others; or

    b.   the protection of national security, public order, or public health or morals.

3. The right of expression may not be restricted by indirect methods or means, such as the abuse of government or private controls over newsprint, radio broadcasting frequencies, or equipment used in the dissemination of information, or by any other means tending to impede the communication and circulation of ideas and opinions.

4. Notwithstanding the provisions of paragraph 2 above, public entertainments may be subject by law to prior censorship for the sole purpose of regulating access to them for the moral protection of childhood and adolescence.

5. Any propaganda for war and any advocacy of national, racial, or religious hatred that constitute incitements to lawless violence or to any other similar action against any person or group of persons on any grounds including those of race, color, religion, language, or national origin shall be considered as offenses punishable by law.

Article 14. Right of Reply

1. Anyone injured by inaccurate or offensive statements or ideas disseminated to the public in general by a legally regulated medium of communication has the right to reply or to make a correction using the same communications outlet, under such conditions as the law may establish.

2. The correction or reply shall not in any case remit other legal liabilities that may have been incurred.

3. For the effective protection of honor and reputation, every publisher, and every newspaper, motion picture, radio, and television company, shall have a person responsible who is not protected by immunities or special privileges.

Article 15. Right of Assembly

The right of peaceful assembly, without arms, is recognized. No restrictions may be placed on the exercise of this right other than those imposed in conformity with the law and necessary in a democratic society in the interest of national security, public safety or public order, or to protect public health or morals or the rights or freedom of others.

Article 16. Freedom of Association

1. Everyone has the right to associate freely for ideological, religious, political, economic, labor, social, cultural, sports, or other purposes.

2. The exercise of this right shall be subject only to such restrictions established by law as may be necessary in a democratic society, in the interest of national security, public safety or public order, or to protect public health or morals or the rights and freedoms of others.

3. The provisions of this article do not bar the imposition of legal restrictions, including even deprivation of the exercise of the right of association, on members of the armed forces and the police.

Article 17. Rights of the Family

1. The family is the natural and fundamental group unit of society and is entitled to protection by society and the state.

2. The right of men and women of marriageable age to marry and to raise a family shall be recognized, if they meet the conditions required by domestic laws, insofar as such conditions do not affect the principle of nondiscrimination established in this Convention.

3. No marriage shall be entered into without the free and full consent of the intending spouses.

4. The States Parties shall take appropriate steps to ensure the equality of rights and the adequate balancing of responsibilities of the spouses as to marriage, during marriage, and in the event of its dissolution. In case of dissolution, provision shall be made for the necessary protection of any children solely on the basis of their own best interests.

5. The law shall recognize equal rights for children born out of wedlock and those born in wedlock.

Article 18. Right to a Name

Every person has the right to a given name and to the surnames of his parents or that of one of them. The law shall regulate the manner in which this right shall be ensured for all, by the use of assumed names if necessary.

Article 19. Rights of the Child

Every minor child has the right to the measures of protection required by his condition as a minor on the part of his family, society, and the state.

Article 20. Right to Nationality

1. Every person has the right to a nationality.

2. Every person has the right to the nationality of the state in whose territory he was born if he does not have the right to any other nationality.

3. No one shall be arbitrarily deprived of his nationality or of the right to change it.

Article 21. Right to Property

1. Everyone has the right to the use and enjoyment of his property. The law may subordinate such use and enjoyment to the interest of society.

2. No one shall be deprived of his property except upon payment of just compensation, for reasons of public utility or social interest, and in the cases and according to the forms established by law.

3. Usury and any other form of exploitation of man by man shall be prohibited by law.

Article 22. Freedom of Movement and Residence

1. Every person lawfully in the territory of a State Party has the right to move about in it, and to reside in it subject to the provisions of the law.

2. Every person has the right to leave any country freely, including his own.

3. The exercise of the foregoing rights may be restricted only pursuant to a law to the extent necessary in a democratic society to prevent crime or to protect national security, public safety, public order, public morals, public health, or the rights or freedoms of others.

4. The exercise of the rights recognized in paragraph 1 may also be restricted by law in designated zones for reasons of public interest.

5. No one can be expelled from the territory of the state of which he is a national or be deprived of the right to enter it.

6. An alien lawfully in the territory of a State Party to this Convention may be expelled from it only pursuant to a decision reached in accordance with law.

7. Every person has the right to seek and be granted asylum in a foreign territory, in accordance with the legislation of the state and international conventions, in the event he is being pursued for political offenses or related common crimes.

8. In no case may an alien be deported or returned to a country, regardless of whether or not it is his country of origin, if in that country his right to life or personal freedom is in danger of being violated because of his race, nationality, religion, social status, or political opinions.

9. The collective expulsion of aliens is prohibited.

Article 23. Right to Participate in Government

1. Every citizen shall enjoy the following rights and opportunities:

    a.   to take part in the conduct of public affairs, directly or through freely chosen representatives;

    b.   to vote and to be elected in genuine periodic elections, which shall be by universal and equal suffrage and by secret ballot that guarantees the free expression of the will of the voters; and

    c.   to have access, under general conditions of equality, to the public service of his country.

2. The law may regulate the exercise of the rights and opportunities referred to in the preceding paragraph only on the basis of age, nationality, residence, language, education, civil and mental capacity, or sentencing by a competent court in criminal proceedings.

Article 24. Right to Equal Protection

All persons are equal before the law. Consequently, they are entitled, without discrimination, to equal protection of the law.

Article 25. Right to Judicial Protection

1. Everyone has the right to simple and prompt recourse, or any other effective recourse, to a competent court or tribunal for protection against

acts that violate his fundamental rights recognized by the constitution or laws of the state concerned or by this Convention, even though such violation may have been committed by persons acting in the course of their official duties.

2. The States Parties undertake:

    a.   to ensure that any person claiming such remedy shall have his rights determined by the competent authority provided for by the legal system of the state;

    b.   to develop the possibilities of judicial remedy; and

    c.   to ensure that the competent authorities shall enforce such remedies when granted.

Chapter III — Economic, Social, and Cultural Rights

Article 26. Progressive Development

The States Parties undertake to adopt measures, both internally and through international cooperation, especially those of an economic and technical nature, with a view to achieving progressively, by legislation or other appropriate means, the full realization of the rights implicit in the economic, social, educational, scientific, and cultural standards set forth in the Charter of the Organization of American States as amended by the Protocol of Buenos Aires.

Chapter IV — Suspension of Guarantees, Interpretation, and Application

Article 27. Suspension of Guarantees

1. In time of war, public danger, or other emergency that threatens the independence or security of a State Party, it may take measures derogating from its obligations under the present Convention to the extent and for the period of time strictly required by the exigencies of the situation, provided that such measures are not inconsistent with its other obligations under international law and do not involve discrimination on the ground of race, color, sex, language, religion, or social origin.

2. The foregoing provision does not authorize any suspension of the following articles: Article 3 (Right to Juridical Personality), Article 4 (Right to Life), Article 5 (Right to Humane Treatment), Article 6 (Freedom from Slavery), Article 9 (Freedom from Ex Post Facto Laws), Article 12 (Freedom of Conscience and Religion), Article 17 (Rights of the Family), Article 18 (Right to a Name), Article 19 (Rights of the Child),

Article 20 (Right to Nationality), and Article 23 (Right to Participate in Government), or of the judicial guarantees essential for the protection of such rights.

3. Any State Party availing itself of the right of suspension shall immediately inform the other States Parties, through the Secretary General of the Organization of American States, of the provisions the application of which it has suspended, the reasons that gave rise to the suspension, and the date set for the termination of such suspension.

Article 28. Federal Clause

1. Where a State Party is constituted as a federal state, the national government of such State Party shall implement all the provisions of the Convention over whose subject matter it exercises legislative and judicial jurisdiction.

2. With respect to the provisions over whose subject matter the constituent units of the federal state have jurisdiction, the national government shall immediately take suitable measures, in accordance with its constitution and its laws, to the end that the competent authorities of the constituent units may adopt appropriate provisions for the fulfillment of this Convention.

3. Whenever two or more States Parties agree to form a federation or other type of association, they shall take care that the resulting federal or other compact contains the provisions necessary for continuing and rendering effective the standards of this Convention in the new state that is organized.

Article 29. Restrictions Regarding Interpretation

No provision of this Convention shall be interpreted as:

    a.   permitting any State Party, group, or person to suppress the enjoyment or exercise of the rights and freedoms recognized in this Convention or to restrict them to a greater extent than is provided for herein;

    b.   restricting the enjoyment or exercise of any right or freedom recognized by virtue of the laws of any State Party or by virtue of another convention to which one of the said states is a party;

    c.   precluding other rights or guarantees that are inherent in the human personality or derived from representative democracy as a form of government; or

d.   excluding or limiting the effect that the American Declaration of the Rights and Duties of Man and other international acts of the same nature may have.

Article 30. Scope of Restrictions

The restrictions that, pursuant to this Convention, may be placed on the enjoyment or exercise of the rights or freedoms recognized herein may not be applied except in accordance with laws enacted for reasons of general interest and in accordance with the purpose for which such restrictions have been established.

Article 31. Recognition of Other Rights

Other rights and freedoms recognized in accordance with the procedures established in Articles 76 and 77 may be included in the system of protection of this Convention.

Chapter V — Personal Responsibilities

Article 32. Relationship between Duties and Rights

1. Every person has responsibilities to his family, his community, and mankind.

2. The rights of each person are limited by the rights of others, by the security of all, and by the just demands of the general welfare, in a democratic society.

III. CANADIAN

(a) Constitutional

1.   Canadian Charter of Rights and Freedoms

Part I of the Constitution Act, 1982, being Schedule B to the Canada Act 1982 (U.K.), 1982, c. 11.

Part I

Canadian Charter of Rights and Freedoms

Whereas Canada is founded upon principles that recognize the supremacy of God and the rule of law:

Guarantee of Rights and Freedoms

1. The *Canadian Charter of Rights and Freedoms* guarantees the rights and freedoms set out in it subject only to such reasonable limits prescribed by law as can be demonstrably justified in a free and democratic society.

Fundamental Freedoms

2. Everyone has the following fundamental freedoms:

(*a*) freedom of conscience and religion;

(*b*) freedom of thought, belief, opinion and expression, including freedom of the press and other media of communication;

(*c*) freedom of peaceful assembly; and

(*d*) freedom of association.

Democratic Rights

3. Every citizen of Canada has the right to vote in an election of members of the House of Commons or of a legislative assembly and to be qualified for membership therein.

4. (1) No House of Commons and no legislative assembly shall continue for longer than five years from the date fixed for the return of the writs of a general election of its members.

(2) In time of real or apprehended war, invasion or insurrection, a House of Commons may be continued by Parliament and a legislative assembly may be continued by the legislature beyond five years if such continuation is not opposed by the votes of more than one-third of the members of the House of Commons or the legislative assembly, as the case may be.

5. There shall be a sitting of Parliament and of each legislature at least once every twelve months.

Mobility Rights

6. (1) Every citizen of Canada has the right to enter, remain in and leave Canada.

(2) Every citizen of Canada and every person who has the status of a permanent resident of Canada has the right

(*a*) to move to and take up residence in any province; and

(*b*) to pursue the gaining of a livelihood in any province.

(3) The rights specified in subsection (2) are subject to

(*a*) any laws or practices of general application in force in a province other than those that discriminate among persons primarily on the basis of province of present or previous residence; and

(*b*) any laws providing for reasonable residency requirements as a qualification for the receipt of publicly provided social services.

(4) Subsections (2) and (3) do not preclude any law, program or activity that has as its object the amelioration in a province of conditions of individuals in that province who are socially or economically disadvantaged if the rate of employment in that province is below the rate of employment in Canada.

Legal Rights

7. Everyone has the right to life, liberty and security of the person and the right not to be deprived thereof except in accordance with the principles of fundamental justice.

8. Everyone has the right to be secure against unreasonable search or seizure.

9. Everyone has the right not to be arbitrarily detained or imprisoned.

10. Everyone has the right on arrest or detention

(*a*) to be informed promptly of the reasons therefor;

(*b*) to retain and instruct counsel without delay and to be informed of that right; and

(*c*) to have the validity of the detention determined by way of *habeas corpus* and to be released if the detention is not lawful.

11. Any person charged with an offence has the right

(*a*) to be informed without unreasonable delay of the specific offence;

(*b*) to be tried within a reasonable time;

(*c*) not to be compelled to be a witness in proceedings against that person in respect of the offence;

(*d*) to be presumed innocent until proven guilty according to law in a fair and public hearing by an independent and impartial tribunal;

(*e*) not to be denied reasonable bail without just cause;

(*f*) except in the case of an offence under military law tried before a military tribunal, to the benefit of trial by jury where the maximum punishment for the offence is imprisonment for five years or a more severe punishment;

(*g*) not to be found guilty on account of any act or omission unless, at the time of the act or omission, it constituted an offence under Canadian or international law or was criminal according to the general principles of law recognized by the community of nations;

(*h*) if finally acquitted of the offence, not to be tried for it again and, if finally found guilty and punished for the offence, not to be tried or punished for it again; and

(*i*) if found guilty of the offence and if the punishment for the offence has been varied between the time of commission and the time of sentencing, to the benefit of the lesser punishment.

12. Everyone has the right not to be subjected to any cruel and unusual treatment or punishment.

13. A witness who testifies in any proceedings has the right not to have any incriminating evidence so given used to incriminate that witness in any other proceedings, except in a prosecution for perjury or for the giving of contradictory evidence.

14. A party or witness in any proceedings who does not understand or speak the language in which the proceedings are conducted or who is deaf has the right to the assistance of an interpreter.

Equality Rights

15. (1) Every individual is equal before and under the law and has the right to the equal protection and equal benefit of the law without discrimination and, in particular, without discrimination based on race, national or ethnic origin, colour, religion, sex, age or mental or physical disability.

(2) Subsection (1) does not preclude any law, program or activity that has as its object the amelioration of conditions of disadvantaged individuals or groups including those that are disadvantaged because of race, national or ethnic origin, colour, religion, sex, age or mental or physical disability.

Official Languages of Canada

16. (1) English and French are the official languages of Canada and have equality of status and equal rights and privileges as to their use in all institutions of the Parliament and government of Canada.

(2) English and French are the official languages of New Brunswick and have equality of status and equal rights and privileges as to their use in all institutions of the legislature and government of New Brunswick.

(3) Nothing in this Charter limits the authority of Parliament or a legislature to advance the equality of status or use of English and French.

16.1 (1) The English linguistic community and the French linguistic community in New Brunswick have equality of status and equal rights and privileges, including the right to distinct educational institutions and such distinct cultural institutions as are necessary for the preservation and promotion of those communities.

(2) The role of the legislature and government of New Brunswick to preserve and promote the status, rights and privileges referred to in subsection (1) is affirmed.

17. (1) Everyone has the right to use English or French in any debates and other proceedings of Parliament.

(2) Everyone has the right to use English or French in any debates and other proceedings of the legislature of New Brunswick.

18. (1) The statutes, records and journals of Parliament shall be printed and published in English and French and both language versions are equally authoritative.

(2) The statutes, records and journals of the legislature of New Brunswick shall be printed and published in English and French and both language versions are equally authoritative.

19. (1) Either English or French may be used by any person in, or in any pleading in or process issuing from, any court established by Parliament.

(2) Either English or French may be used by any person in, or in any pleading in or process issuing from, any court of New Brunswick.

20. (1) Any member of the public in Canada has the right to communicate with, and to receive available services from, any head or central office of an institution of the Parliament or government of Canada in English or French, and has the same right with respect to any other office of any such institution where

(a) there is a significant demand for communications with and services from that office in such language; or

(b) due to the nature of the office, it is reasonable that communications with and services from that office be available in both English and French.

(2) Any member of the public in New Brunswick has the right to communicate with, and to receive available services from, any office of an institution of the legislature or government of New Brunswick in English or French.

21. Nothing in sections 16 to 20 abrogates or derogates from any right, privilege or obligation with respect to the English and French languages, or either of them, that exists or is continued by virtue of any other provision of the Constitution of Canada.

22. Nothing in sections 16 to 20 abrogates or derogates from any legal or customary right or privilege acquired or enjoyed either before or after the coming into force of this Charter with respect to any language that is not English or French.

Minority Language Educational Rights

23. (1) Citizens of Canada

(a) whose first language learned and still understood is that of the English or French linguistic minority population of the province in which they reside, or

(b) who have received their primary school instruction in Canada in English or French and reside in a province where the language in which they received that instruction is the language of the English or French linguistic minority population of the province,

have the right to have their children receive primary and secondary school instruction in that language in that province.

(2) Citizens of Canada of whom any child has received or is receiving primary or secondary school instruction in English or French in Canada, have the right to have all their children receive primary and secondary school instruction in the same language.

(3) The right of citizens of Canada under subsections (1) and (2) to have their children receive primary and secondary school instruction in the language of the English or French linguistic minority population of a province

(a) applies wherever in the province the number of children of citizens who have such a right is sufficient to warrant the provision to them out of public funds of minority language instruction; and

(b) includes, where the number of those children so warrants, the right to have them receive that instruction in minority language educational facilities provided out of public funds.

Enforcement

24. (1) Anyone whose rights or freedoms, as guaranteed by this Charter, have been infringed or denied may apply to a court of competent jurisdiction to obtain such remedy as the court considers appropriate and just in the circumstances.

(2) Where, in proceedings under subsection (1), a court concludes that evidence was obtained in a manner that infringed or denied any rights or freedoms guaranteed by this Charter, the evidence shall be excluded if it is established that, having regard to all the circumstances, the admission of it in the proceedings would bring the administration of justice into disrepute.

General

25. The guarantee in this Charter of certain rights and freedoms shall not be construed so as to abrogate or derogate from any aboriginal, treaty or other rights or freedoms that pertain to the aboriginal peoples of Canada including

(a) any rights or freedoms that have been recognized by the Royal Proclamation of October 7, 1763; and

(b) any rights or freedoms that now exist by way of land claims agreements or may be so acquired.

26. The guarantee in this Charter of certain rights and freedoms shall not be construed as denying the existence of any other rights or freedoms that exist in Canada.

27. This Charter shall be interpreted in a manner consistent with the preservation and enhancement of the multicultural heritage of Canadians.

28. Notwithstanding anything in this Charter, the rights and freedoms referred to in it are guaranteed equally to male and female persons.

29. Nothing in this Charter abrogates or derogates from any rights or privileges guaranteed by or under the Constitution of Canada in respect of denominational, separate or dissentient schools.

30. A reference in this Charter to a Province or to the legislative assembly or legislature of a province shall be deemed to include a reference to the Yukon Territory and the Northwest Territories, or to the appropriate legislative authority thereof, as the case may be.

31. Nothing in this Charter extends the legislative powers of any body or authority.

Application of Charter

32. (1) This Charter applies

(a) to the Parliament and government of Canada in respect of all matters within the authority of Parliament including all matters relating to the Yukon Territory and Northwest Territories; and

(b) to the legislature and government of each province in respect of all matters within the authority of the legislature of each province.

(2) Notwithstanding subsection (1), section 15 shall not have effect until three years after this section comes into force.

33. (1) Parliament or the legislature of a province may expressly declare in an Act of Parliament or of the legislature, as the case may be, that the Act or a provision thereof shall operate notwithstanding a provision included in section 2 or sections 7 to 15 of this Charter.

(2) An Act or a provision of an Act in respect of which a declaration made under this section is in effect shall have such operation as it would have but for the provision of this Charter referred to in the declaration.

(3) A declaration made under subsection (1) shall cease to have effect five years after it comes into force or on such earlier date as may be specified in the declaration.

(4) Parliament or the legislature of a province may re-enact a declaration made under subsection (1).

(5) Subsection (3) applies in respect of a re-enactment made under subsection (4).

Citation

34. This Part may be cited as the Canadian Charter of Rights and Freedoms.

(b)   Federal Legislation

(i)   Human Rights Statutes

1.   Canadian Bill of Rights

S.C. 1960, c. 44.

An Act for the Recognition and Protection of Human Rights and Fundamental Freedoms

The Parliament of Canada, affirming that the Canadian Nation is founded upon principles that acknowledge the supremacy of God, the dignity and worth of the human person and the position of the family in a society of free men and free institutions;

Affirming also that men and institutions remain free only when freedom is founded upon respect for moral and spiritual values and the rule of law;

And being desirous of enshrining these principles and the human rights and fundamental freedoms derived from them, in a Bill of Rights which shall reflect the respect of Parliament for its constitutional authority and which shall ensure the protection of these rights and freedoms in Canada:

Therefore Her Majesty, by and with the advice and consent of the Senate and House of Commons of Canada, enacts as follows:

Part I

Bill of Rights

1. It is hereby recognized and declared that in Canada there have existed and shall continue to exist without discrimination by reason of race, national origin, colour, religion or sex, the following human rights and fundamental freedoms, namely,

> (*a*) the right of the individual to life, liberty, security of the person and enjoyment of property, and the right not to be deprived thereof except by due process of law;
>
> (*b*) the right of the individual to equality before the law and the protection of the law;
>
> (*c*) freedom of religion;
>
> (*d*) freedom of speech;
>
> (*e*) freedom of assembly and association; and
>
> (*f*) freedom of the press.

2. Every law of Canada shall, unless it is expressly declared by an Act of the Parliament of Canada that it shall operate notwithstanding the *Canadian Bill of Rights*, be so construed and applied as not to abrogate, abridge or infringe or to authorize the abrogation, abridgment or infringement of any of the rights or freedoms herein recognized and declared, and in particular, no law of Canada shall be construed or applied so as to

> (*a*) authorize or effect the arbitrary detention, imprisonment or exile of any person;
>
> (*b*) impose or authorize the imposition of cruel and unusual treatment or punishment;
>
> (*c*) deprive a person who has been arrested or detained
>
> > (i) of the right to be informed promptly of the reason for his arrest or detention,
> >
> > (ii) of the right to retain and instruct counsel without delay, or
> >
> > (iii) of the remedy by way of habeas corpus for the determination of the validity of his detention and for his release if the detention is not lawful;

(*d*) authorize a court, tribunal, commission, board or other authority to compel a person to give evidence if he is denied counsel, protection against self crimination or other constitutional safeguards;

(*e*) deprive a person of the right to a fair hearing in accordance with the principles of fundamental justice for the determination of his rights and obligations;

(*f*) deprive a person charged with a criminal offence of the right to be presumed innocent until proved guilty according to law in a fair and public hearing by an independent and impartial tribunal, or of the right to reasonable bail without just cause; or

(*g*) deprive a person of the right to the assistance of an interpreter in any proceedings in which he is involved or in which he is a party or a witness, before a court, commission, board or other tribunal, if he does not understand or speak the language in which such proceedings are conducted.

3. (1) Subject to subsection (2), the Minister of Justice shall, in accordance with such regulations as may be prescribed by the Governor in Council, examine every regulation transmitted to the Clerk of the Privy Council for registration pursuant to the *Statutory Instruments Act* and every Bill introduced in or presented to the House of Commons by a Minister of the Crown, in order to ascertain whether any of the provisions thereof are inconsistent with the purposes and provisions of this Part and he shall report any such inconsistency to the House of Commons at the first convenient opportunity.

(2) A regulation need not be examined in accordance with subsection (1) if prior to being made it was examined as a proposed regulation in accordance with section 3 of the *Statutory Instruments Act* to ensure that it was not inconsistent with the purposes and provisions of this Part.

[1960, c. 44, s. 3; 1970-71-72, c. 38, s. 29; 1985, c. 26, s. 105; 1992, c. 1, s. 144 (F)]

4. The provisions of this Part shall be known as the *Canadian Bill of Rights*.

Part II

5. (1) Nothing in Part I shall be construed to abrogate or abridge any human right or fundamental freedom not enumerated therein that may have existed in Canada at the commencement of this Act.

(2) The expression "law of Canada" in Part I means an Act of the Parliament of Canada enacted before or after the coming into force of this Act, any order, rule or regulation thereunder, and any law in force in

Canada or in any part of Canada at the commencement of this Act that is subject to be repealed, abolished or altered by the Parliament of Canada.

(3) The provisions of Part I shall be construed as extending only to matters coming within the legislative authority of the Parliament of Canada.

2.   Canadian Human Rights Act

R.S.C. 1985, c. H-6.

An Act to extend the laws in Canada that proscribe discrimination

SHORT TITLE

1. Short title — This Act may be cited as the *Canadian Human Rights Act.*

[1976-77, c. 33, s. 1]

PURPOSE OF ACT

2. Purpose — The purpose of this Act is to extend the laws in Canada to give effect, within the purview of matters coming within the legislative authority of Parliament, to the principle that all individuals should have an opportunity equal with other individuals to make for themselves the lives that they are able and wish to have and to have their needs accommodated, consistent with their duties and obligations as members of society, without being hindered in or prevented from doing so by discriminatory practices based on race, national or ethnic origin, colour, religion, age, sex, sexual orientation, marital status, family status, disability or conviction for an offence for which a pardon has been granted.

[1996, c. 14, s. 1; 1998, c. 9, s. 9]

PART I

PROSCRIBED DISCRIMINATION

GENERAL

3. Proscribed grounds of discrimination — (1) For all purposes of this Act, the prohibited grounds of discrimination are race, national or ethnic origin, colour, religion, age, sex, sexual orientation, marital status, family status, disability and conviction for which a pardon has been granted.

[1996, c. 14, s. 2]

(2) Idem — Where the ground of discrimination is pregnancy or child-birth, the discrimination shall be deemed to be on the ground of sex.

3.1. Multiple grounds of discrimination — For greater certainty, a discriminatory practice includes a practice based on one or more prohibited grounds of discrimination or on the effect of a combination of prohibited grounds.

[1998, c. 9, s. 11]

4. Orders regarding discriminatory practices — A discriminatory practice, as described in sections 5 to 14.1, may be the subject of a complaint under Part III and anyone found to be engaging or to have engaged in a discriminatory practice may be made subject to an order as provided in sections 53 and 54.

[1998, c. 9, s. 11]

DISCRIMINATORY PRACTICES

5. Denial of good, service, facility or accommodation — It is a discriminatory practice in the provision of goods, services, facilities or accommodation customarily available to the general public

(*a*) to deny, or to deny access to, any such good, service, facility or accommodation to any individual, or

(*b*) to differentiate adversely in relation to any individual,

on a prohibited ground of discrimination.

[1976-77, c. 33, s. 5]

6. Denial of commercial premises or residential accommodation — It is a discriminatory practice in the provision of commercial premises or residential accommodation

(*a*) to deny occupancy of such premises or accommodation to any individual, or

(*b*) to differentiate adversely in relation to any individual,

on a prohibited ground of discrimination.

[1976-77, c. 33, s. 6]

7. Employment — It is a discriminatory practice, directly or indirectly,

(*a*) to refuse to employ or continue to employ any individual, or

(*b*) in the course of employment, to differentiate adversely in relation to an employee,

on a prohibited ground of discrimination.

[1976-77, c. 33, s. 7]

8. Employment applications, advertisements — It is a discriminatory practice

(a) to use or circulate any form of application for employment, or

(b) in connection with employment or prospective employment, to publish any advertisement or to make any written or oral inquiry

that expresses or implies any limitation, specification or preference based on a prohibited ground of discrimination.

[1976-77, c. 33, s. 8]

9. Employee organizations — (1) It is a discriminatory practice for an employee organization on a prohibited ground of discrimination

(a) to exclude an individual from full membership in the organization;

(b) to expel or suspend a member of the organization; or

(c) to limit, segregate, classify or otherwise act in relation to an individual in a way that would deprive the individual of employment opportunities, or limit employment opportunities or otherwise adversely affect the status of the individual, where the individual is a member of the organization or where any of the obligations of the organization pursuant to a collective agreement relate to the individual.

(2) **Exception** — Notwithstanding subsection (1), it is not a discriminatory practice for an employee organization to exclude, expel or suspend an individual from membership in the organization because that individual has reached the normal age of retirement for individuals working in positions similar to the position of that individual.

(3) [Repealed: 1998, c. 9, s. 12]

[1998, c. 9, s. 12]

10. Discriminatory policy or practice — It is a discriminatory practice for an employer, employee organization or employer organization

(a) to establish or pursue a policy or practice, or

(b) to enter into an agreement affecting recruitment, referral, hiring, promotion, training, apprenticeship, transfer or any other matter relating to employment or prospective employment,

that deprives or tends to deprive an individual or class of individuals of any employment opportunities on a prohibited ground of discrimination.

[1988, c. 9, s. 13]

11. Equal wages — (1) It is a discriminatory practice for an employer to establish or maintain differences in wages between male and female employees employed in the same establishment who are performing work of equal value.

(2) **Assessment of value of work** — In assessing the value of work performed by employees employed in the same establishment, the criterion to be applied is the composite of the skill, effort and responsibility required in the performance of the work and the conditions under which the work is performed.

(3) **Separate establishments** — Separate establishments established or maintained by an employer solely or principally for the purpose of establishing or maintaining differences in wages between male and female employees shall be deemed for the purposes of this section to be the same establishment.

(4) **Different wages based on prescribed reasonable factors** — Notwithstanding subsection (1), it is not a discriminatory practice to pay male and female employees different wages if the difference is based on a factor prescribed by guidelines, issued by the Canadian Human Rights Commission pursuant to subsection 27(2), to be a reasonable factor that justifies the difference.

(5) **Idem** — For greater certainty, sex does not constitute a reasonable factor justifying a difference in wages.

(6) **No reduction of wages** — An employer shall not reduce wages in order to eliminate a discriminatory practice described in this section.

(7) **Definition of "wages"** — For the purposes of this section, "wages" means any form of remuneration payable for work performed by an individual and includes

(*a*) salaries, commissions, vacation pay, dismissal wages and bonuses;

(*b*) reasonable value for board, rent, housing and lodging;

(*c*) payments in kind;

(*d*) employer contributions to pension funds or plans, long-term disability plans and all forms of health insurance plans; and

(*e*) any other advantage received directly or indirectly from the individual's employer.

[1976-77, c. 33, s. 11]

12. Publication of discriminatory notices, etc. — It is a discriminatory practice to publish or display before the public or to cause to be

published or displayed before the public any notice, sign, symbol, emblem
or other representation that

(*a*) expresses or implies discrimination or an intention to discriminate,
or

(*b*) incites or is calculated to incite others to discriminate

if the discrimination expressed or implied, intended to be expressed or
implied or incited or calculated to be incited would otherwise, if engaged
in, be a discriminatory practice described in any of sections 5 to 11 or in
section 14.

[1976-77, c. 33, s. 12; 1980-81-82-83, c. 143, s. 6]

13. Hate messages — (1) It is a discriminatory practice for a person or
a group of persons acting in concert to communicate telephonically or to
cause to be so communicated, repeatedly, in whole or in part by means of
the facilities of a telecommunication undertaking within the legislative
authority of Parliament, any matter that is likely to expose a person or
persons to hatred or contempt by reason of the fact that that person or
those persons are identifiable on the basis of a prohibited ground of
discrimination.

(2) **Interpretation** — For greater certainty, subsection (1) applies in
respect of a matter that is communicated by means of a computer or a
group of interconnected or related computers, including the Internet, or
any similar means of communication, but does not apply in respect of a
matter that is communicated in whole or in part by means of the facilities
of a broadcasting undertaking.

(3) **Interpretation** — For the purposes of this section, no owner or
operator of a telecommunication undertaking communicates or causes to
be communicated any matter described in subsection (1) by reason only
that the facilities of a telecommunication undertaking owned or operated
by that person are used by other persons for the transmission of that
matter.

[1976-77, c. 33, s. 13; 2001, c. 41, s. 88]

14. Harassment — (1) It is a discriminatory practice,

(*a*) in the provision of goods, services, facilities or accommodation
customarily available to the general public,

(*b*) in the provision of commercial premises or residential accommodation, or

(*c*) in matters related to employment,

to harass an individual on a prohibited ground of discrimination.

(2) **Sexual harassment** — Without limiting the generality of subsection (1), sexual harassment shall, for the purposes of that subsection, be deemed to be harassment on a prohibited ground of discrimination.

[1980-81-82-83, c. 143, s. 7]

14.1 Retaliation — It is a discriminatory practice for a person against whom a complaint has been filed under Part III, or any person acting on their behalf, to retaliate or threaten retaliation against the individual who filed the complaint or the alleged victim.

[1988, c. 9, s. 14]

15. Exceptions — (1) It is not a discriminatory practice if

(*a*) any refusal, exclusion, expulsion, suspension, limitation, specification or preference in relation to any employment is established by an employer to be based on a *bona fide* occupational requirement;

(*b*) employment of an individual is refused or terminated because that individual has not reached the minimum age, or has reached the maximum age, that applies to that employment by law or under regulations, which may be made by the Governor in Council for the purposes of this paragraph;

(*c*) an individual's employment is terminated because that individual has reached the normal age of retirement for employees working in positions similar to the position of that individual;

(*d*) the terms and conditions of any pension fund or plan established by an employer, employee organization or employer organization provide for the compulsory vesting or locking-in of pension contributions at a fixed or determinable age in accordance with sections 17 and 18 of the *Pension Benefits Standards Act, 1985*;

(*e*) an individual is discriminated against on a prohibited ground of discrimination in a manner that is prescribed by guidelines, issued by the Canadian Human Rights Commission pursuant to subsection 27(2), to be reasonable;

(*f*) an employer, employee organization or employer organization grants a female employee special leave or benefits in connection with pregnancy or child-birth or grants employees special leave or benefits to assist them in the care of their children; or

(*g*) in the circumstances described in section 5 or 6, an individual is denied any goods, services, facilities or accommodation or access thereto or occupancy of any commercial premises or residential accommodation or is a victim of any adverse differentiation and there is *bona fide* justification for that denial or differentiation.

(2) **Accommodation of needs** — For any practice mentioned in paragraph (1)(*a*) to be considered to be based on a *bona fide* occupational requirement and for any practice mentioned in paragraph (1)(*g*) to be considered to have a *bona fide* justification, it must be established that accommodation of the needs of an individual or a class of individuals affected would impose undue hardship on the person who would have to accommodate those needs, considering health, safety and cost.

(3) **Regulations** — The Governor in Council may make regulations prescribing standards for assessing undue hardship.

(4) **Publication of proposed regulations** — Each regulation that the Governor in Council proposes to make under subsection (3) shall be published in the *Canada Gazette* and a reasonable opportunity shall be given to interested persons to make representations in respect of it.

(5) **Consultations** — The Canadian Human Rights Commission shall conduct public consultations concerning any regulation proposed to be made by the Governor in Council under subsection (3) and shall file a report of the results of the consultations with the Minister within a reasonable time after the publication of the proposed regulation in the *Canada Gazette.*

(6) **Exception** — A proposed regulation need not be published more than once, whether or not it has been amended as a result of any representations.

(7) **Making of regulations** — The Governor in Council may proceed to make regulations under subsection (3) after six months have elapsed since the publication of the proposed regulations in the *Canada Gazette,* whether or not a report described in subsection (5) is filed.

(8) **Application** — This section applies in respect of a practice regardless of whether it results in direct discrimination or adverse effect discrimination.

(9) **Universality of Service for Canadian Forces** — Subsection (2) is subject to the principle of universality of service under which members of the Canadian Forces must at all times and under any circumstances perform any functions that they may be required to perform.

[1985, c. 32 (2nd Supp.), s. 41; 1998, c. 9, s. 10; 1998, c. 9, s. 15]

16. Special Programs — (1) It is not a discriminatory practice for a person to adopt or carry out a special program, plan or arrangement designed to prevent disadvantages that are likely to be suffered by, or to eliminate or reduce disadvantages that are suffered by, any group of individuals when those disadvantages would be based on or related to the prohibited grounds of discrimination, by improving opportunities respecting goods, services, facilities, accommodation or employment in relation to that group.

(2) **Advice and assistance** — The Canadian Human Rights Commission, may

    (*a*) make general recommendations concerning desirable objectives for special programs, plans or arrangements referred to in subsection (1); and

    (*b*) on application, give such advice and assistance with respect to the adoption or carrying out of a special program, plan or arrangement referred to in subsection (1) as will serve to aid in the achievement of the objectives the program, plan or arrangement was designed to achieve.

(3) It is not a discriminatory practice to collect information relating to a prohibited ground of discrimination if the information is intended to be used in adopting or carrying out a special program, plan or arrangement under subsection (1).

[1998, c. 9, s. 16]

17. Plans to meet the needs of disabled persons — (1) A person who proposes to implement a plan for adapting any services, facilities, premises, equipment or operations to meet the needs of persons arising from a disability may apply to the Canadian Human Rights Commission for approval of the plan.

(2) **Approval of Plan** — The Commission may, by written notice to a person making an application pursuant to subsection (1), approve the plan if the Commission is satisfied that the plan is appropriate for meeting the needs of persons arising from a disability.

(3) **Effect of approval of accommodation plan** — Where any services, facilities, premises, equipment or operations are adapted in accordance with a plan approved under subsection (2), matters for which the plan provides do not constitute any basis for a complaint under Part III regarding discrimination based on any disability in respect of which the plan was approved.

(4) **Notice when application not granted** — When the Commission decides not to grant an application made pursuant to subsection (1), it shall send a written notice of its decision to the applicant setting out the reasons for its decision.

[1980-81-82-83, c. 143, s. 9]

18. Rescinding approval of plan — (1) If the Canadian Human Rights Commission is satisfied that, by reason of any change in circumstances, a plan approved under subsection 17(2) has ceased to be appropriate for meeting the needs of persons arising from a disability, the Commission may, by written notice to the person who proposes to carry out or maintains the adaptation contemplated by the plan or any part thereof, rescind its approval of the plan to the extent required by the change in circumstances.

(2) **Effect where approval rescinded** — To the extent to which approval of a plan is rescinded under subsection (1), subsection 17(3) does not apply to the plan if the discriminatory practice to which the complaint relates is subsequent to the rescission of the approval.

(3) **Statement of reasons for rescinding approval** — Where the Commission rescinds approval of a plan pursuant to subsection (1), it shall include in the notice referred to therein a statement of its reasons therefor.

[1980-81-82-83, c. 143, s. 9]

19. Opportunity to make representations — (1) Before making its decision on an application or rescinding approval of a plan pursuant to section 17 or 18, the Canadian Human Rights Commission shall afford each person directly concerned with the matter an opportunity to make representations with respect thereto.

(2) **Restriction on deeming plan inappropriate** — For the purposes of sections 17 and 18, a plan shall not, by reason only that it does not conform to any standards prescribed pursuant to section 24, be deemed to be inappropriate for meeting the needs of persons arising from disability.

[1980-81-82-83, c. 143, s. 9]

20. Certain provisions not discriminatory — A provision of a pension or insurance fund or plan that preserves rights acquired before March 1, 1978 or that preserves pension or other benefits accrued before that day does not constitute the basis for a complaint under Part III that an employer, employee organization or employer organization is engaging or has engaged in a discriminatory practice.

[1998, c. 9, s. 17]

21. Funds and plans — The establishment of separate pension funds or plans for different groups of employees does not constitute the basis for a complaint under Part III that an employer, employee organization or employer organization is engaging or has engaged in a discriminatory practice if the employees are not grouped in those funds or plans according to a prohibited ground of discrimination.

[1998, c. 9, s. 17]

22. Regulations — The Governor in Council may, by regulation, prescribe the provisions of any pension or insurance fund or plan, in addition to the provisions described in sections 20 and 21, that do not constitute the basis for a complaint under Part III that an employer, employee organization or employer organization is engaging or has engaged in a discriminatory practice.

[1998, c. 9, s. 17]

23. Regulations — The Governor in Council may make regulations respecting the terms and conditions to be included in or applicable to any contract, licence or grant made or granted by Her Majesty in right of Canada providing for

(*a*) the prohibition of discriminatory practices described in sections 5 to 14.1; and

(*b*) the resolution, by the procedure set out in Part III, of complaints of discriminatory practices contrary to such terms and conditions.

[1988, c. 9, s. 18]

24. Accessibility standards — (1) The Governor in Council may, for the benefit of persons having any disability, make regulations prescribing standards of accessibility to services, facilities or premises.

(2) Where standards prescribed pursuant to subsection (1) are met in providing access to any services, facilities or premises, a matter of access thereto does not constitute any basis for a complaint under Part III regarding discrimination based on any disability in respect of which the standards are prescribed.

(3) **Publication of proposed regulations** — Subject to subsection (4), a copy of each regulation that the Governor in Council proposes to make pursuant to this section shall be published in the *Canada Gazette* and a reasonable opportunity shall be afforded to interested persons to make representations with respect thereto.

(4) **Exceptions** — Subsection (3) does not apply in respect of a proposed regulation that has been published pursuant to that subsection, whether or not it has been amended as a result of representations made pursuant to that subsection.

(5) **Discriminatory practice not constituted by variance from standards** — Nothing shall, by virtue only of its being at variance with any standards prescribed pursuant to subsection (1), be deemed to constitute a discriminatory practice.

[1980-81-82-83, c. 143, s. 11]

25. Definitions — In this Act,

"conviction for which a pardon has been granted" means a conviction of an individual for an offence in respect of which a pardon has been granted by any authority under law and, if granted or issued under the *Criminal Records Act*, has not been revoked or ceased to have effect;

"disability" means any previous or existing mental or physical disability and includes disfigurement and previous or existing dependence on alcohol or a drug;

"employee organization" includes a trade union or other organization of employees or a local, the purposes of which include the negotiation of terms and conditions of employment on behalf of employees;

"employer organization" means an organization of employers the purposes of which include the regulation of relations between employers and employees;

"employment" includes a contractual relationship with an individual for the provision of services personally by the individual;

"Tribunal" means the Canadian Human Rights Tribunal established by section 48.1.

[1992, c. 22, s. 13; 1998, c. 9, s. 19]

PART II

CANADIAN HUMAN RIGHTS COMMISSION

26. Commission established — (1) A commission is hereby established to be known as the Canadian Human Rights Commission, in this Part and Part III referred to as the "Commission", consisting of a Chief Commissioner, a Deputy Chief Commissioner and not less than three or more than six other members, to be appointed by the Governor in Council.

(2) **Members** — The Chief Commissioner and Deputy Chief Commissioner are full-time members of the Commission and the other members may be appointed as full-time or part-time members of the Commission.

(3) **Term of appointment** — Each full-time member of the Commission may be appointed for a term not exceeding seven years and each part-time member may be appointed for a term not exceeding three years.

(4) **Tenure** — Each member of the Commission holds office during good behaviour but may be removed by the Governor in Council on address of the Senate and House of Commons.

(5) **Re-appointment** — A member of the Commission is eligible to be re-appointed in the same or another capacity.

[1976-77, c. 33, s. 21]

POWERS, DUTIES AND FUNCTIONS

27. Powers, duties and functions — (1) In addition to its duties under Part III with respect to complaints regarding discriminatory practices, the Commission is generally responsible for the administration of this Part and Parts I and III and

(*a*) shall develop and conduct information programs to foster public understanding of this Act and of the role and activities of the Commission thereunder and to foster public recognition of the principle described in section 2;

(*b*) shall undertake or sponsor research programs relating to its duties and functions under this Act and respecting the principle described in section 2;

(*c*) shall maintain close liaison with similar bodies or authorities in the provinces in order to foster common policies and practices and to avoid conflicts respecting the handling of complaints in cases of overlapping jurisdiction;

(*d*) shall perform duties and functions to be performed by it pursuant to any agreement entered into under subsection 28(2);

(*e*) may consider such recommendations, suggestions and requests concerning human rights and freedoms as it receives from any source and, where deemed by the Commission to be appropriate, include in a report referred to in section 61 reference to and comment on any such recommendation, suggestion or request;

(*f*) shall carry out or cause to be carried out such studies concerning human rights and freedoms as may be referred to it by the Minister of Justice and include in a report referred to in section 61 a report setting out the results of each such study together with such recommendations in relation thereto as it considers appropriate;

(*g*) may review any regulations, rules, orders, by-laws and other instruments made pursuant to an Act of Parliament and, where deemed by the Commission to be appropriate, include in a report referred to in section 61 reference to and comment on any provision thereof that in its opinion is inconsistent with the principle described in section 2; and

(*h*) shall, so far as is practical and consistent with the application of Part III, try by persuasion, publicity or any other means that it considers appropriate to discourage and reduce discriminatory practices referred to in sections 5 to 14.1.

(2) **Guidelines** — The Commission may, on application or on its own initiative, by order, issue a guideline setting out the extent to which and the manner in which, in the opinion of the Commission, any provision of this Act applies in a class of cases described in the guideline.

(3) **Guideline binding** — A guideline issued under subsection (2) is, until it is revoked or modified, binding on the Commission and any member or panel assigned under subsection 49(2) with respect to the resolution of a complaint under Part III regarding a case falling within the description contained in the guideline.

(4) **Publication** — Each guideline issued under subsection (2) shall be published in Part II of the *Canada Gazette*.

[1988, c. 9, s. 20]

(ii)   Other Federal Statutes Concerning Human Rights

1.   Canadian Multiculturalism Act

R.S.C. 1985, c. 24 (4th Supp.).

An Act for the preservation and enhancement of multiculturalism in Canada

Preamble

WHEREAS the Constitution of Canada provides that every individual is equal before and under the law and has the right to the equal protection and benefit of the law without discrimination and that everyone has the freedom of conscience, religion, thought, belief, opinion, expression, peaceful assembly and association and guarantees those rights and freedoms equally to male and female persons;

AND WHEREAS the Constitution of Canada recognizes the importance of preserving and enhancing the multicultural heritage of Canadians;

AND WHEREAS the Constitution of Canada recognizes rights of the aboriginal peoples of Canada;

AND WHEREAS the Constitution of Canada and the *Official Languages Act* provide that English and French are the official languages of Canada and neither abrogates nor derogates from any rights or privileges acquired or enjoyed with respect to any other language;

AND WHEREAS the *Citizenship Act* provides that all Canadians, whether by birth or by choice, enjoy equal status, are entitled to the same rights, powers and privileges and are subject to the same obligations, duties and liabilities;

AND WHEREAS the *Canadian Human Rights Act* provides that every individual should have an equal opportunity with other individuals to make the life that the individual is able and wishes to have, consistent with the duties and obligations of that individual as a member of society, and, in order to secure that opportunity, establishes the Canadian Human Rights Commission to redress any proscribed discrimination, including discrimination on the basis of race, national or ethnic origin or colour;

AND WHEREAS Canada is a party to the International Convention on the Elimination of All Forms of Racial Discrimination, which Convention recognizes that all human beings are equal before the law and are entitled to equal protection of the law against any discrimination and against any incitement to discrimination, and to the International Covenant on Civil and Political Rights, which Covenant provides that persons belonging to ethnic, religious or linguistic minorities shall not be denied the right to enjoy their own culture, to profess and practise their own religion or to use their own language;

AND WHEREAS the Government of Canada recognizes the diversity of Canadians as regards race, national or ethnic origin, colour and religion as a fundamental characteristic of Canadian society and is committed to a policy of multiculturalism designed to preserve and enhance the multicultural heritage of Canadians while working to achieve the equality of all Canadians in the economic, social, cultural and political life of Canada;

NOW, THEREFORE, Her Majesty, by and with the advice and consent of the Senate and House of Commons of Canada, enacts as follows:

...

MULTICULTURALISM POLICY OF CANADA

3. Multiculturalism policy — (1) It is hereby declared to be the policy of the Government of Canada to

...

(*e*) ensure that all individuals receive equal treatment and equal protection under the law, while respecting and valuing their diversity; ...

2.   Department of Canadian Heritage Act

S.C. 1995, c. 11.

An Act to establish the Department of Canadian Heritage and to amend and repeal certain other Acts.

POWERS, DUTIES AND FUNCTIONS OF THE MINISTER

4. Minister's powers, duties and functions — (1) The powers, duties and functions of the Minister extend to and include all matters over which Parliament has jurisdiction, not by law assigned to any other department, board or agency of the Government of Canada, relating to Canadian identity and values, cultural development, and heritage.

(2) **Idem** — The Minister's jurisdiction referred to in subsection (1) encompasses, but is not limited to, jurisdiction over

(*a*) the promotion of a greater understanding of human rights, fundamental freedoms and related values;

(*b*) multiculturalism; ...

[1996, c. 11, s. 4, in force July 12, 1996 (SI/96-68); 2002, c. 18, s. 32(F); 2003, c. 2, s. 37; 2005, c. 2, s. 1]

3.   Employment Equity Act

S.C. 1995, c. 44.

An Act respecting employment equity.

PURPOSE OF ACT

2. Purpose of Act — The purpose of this Act is to achieve equality in the workplace so that no person shall be denied employment opportunities or benefits for reasons unrelated to ability and, in the fulfilment of that goal, to correct the conditions of disadvantage in employment experienced by women, aboriginal peoples, persons with disabilities and members of visible minorities by giving effect to the principle that employment equity means more than treating persons in the same way but also requires special measures and the accommodation of differences.

4.   Immigration and Refugee Protection Act

S.C. 2001, c. 27.

An Act respecting immigration to Canada and the granting of refugee protection to persons who are displaced, persecuted or in danger.

OBJECTIVES AND APPLICATION

3. Objectives — immigration — (1) The objectives of this Act with respect to immigration are

...

  (*i*) to promote international justice and security by fostering respect for human rights and by denying access to Canadian territory to persons who are criminals or security risks; and

(2) **Objectives — refugees —** The objectives of this Act with respect to refugees are

...

  (*b*) to fulfil Canada's international legal obligations with respect to refugees and affirm Canada's commitment to international efforts to provide assistance to those in need of resettlement;

  (*c*) to grant, as a fundamental expression of Canada's humanitarian ideals, fair consideration to those who come to Canada claiming persecution;

  (*d*) to offer safe haven to persons with a well-founded fear of persecution based on race, religion, nationality, political opinion or membership in a particular social group, as well as those at risk of torture or cruel and unusual treatment or punishment;

  (*e*) to establish fair and efficient procedures that will maintain the integrity of the Canadian refugee protection system, while upholding Canada's respect for the human rights and fundamental freedoms of all human beings;

...

(3) **Application —** This Act is to be construed and applied in a manner that

  (*a*) furthers the domestic and international interests of Canada;

(*b*) promotes accountability and transparency by enhancing public awareness of immigration and refugee programs;

(*c*) facilitates cooperation between the Government of Canada, provincial governments, foreign states, international organizations and non-governmental organizations;

(*d*) ensures that decisions taken under this Act are consistent with the *Canadian Charter of Rights and Freedoms*, including its principles of equality and freedom from discrimination and of the equality of English and French as the official languages of Canada;

(*e*) supports the commitment of the Government of Canada to enhance the vitality of the English and French linguistic minority communities in Canada; and

(*f*) complies with international human rights instruments to which Canada is signatory.

5.   International Centre for Human Rights and Democratic Development Act

R.S.C. 1985, c. 54 (4th Supp.).

An Act to establish the International Centre for Human Rights and Democratic Development.

OBJECTS, POWERS AND CAPACITY OF CENTRE

4. Objects of Centre — (1) The objects of the Centre are to initiate, encourage and support cooperation between Canada and other countries in the promotion, development and strengthening of democratic and human rights institutions and programs that give effect to the rights and freedoms enshrined in the *International Bill of Human Rights*, including, among those rights,

(*a*) the right to an adequate standard of living;

(*b*) the rights of persons not to be subjected to torture or to cruel, inhuman or degrading treatment or punishment;

(*c*) the rights of freedom of opinion and expression; and

(*d*) the right to vote and be elected at periodic, genuine elections in pluralistic political systems.

(2) **Major object** — A major object of the Centre is to help reduce the wide gap that sometimes exists between the formal adherence of states to international human rights agreements and the actual human rights practices of those states.

(3) **Mandate** — In carrying out its objects, the Centre shall

(*a*) support developmental programs and activities for the benefit of developing countries;

(*b*) support programs and activities for the benefit of countries other than developing countries; and

(*c*) foster and support research and education, discourse, the exchange of information and collaboration among people and institutions in Canada and other countries.

(c)   Provincial and Territorial Legislation

(i)   Bills of Rights

1.   Alberta Bill of Rights

R.S.A. 2000, c. A-14.

Preamble

WHEREAS the free and democratic society existing in Alberta is founded on principles that acknowledge the supremacy of God and on principles, fostered by tradition, that honour and respect human rights and fundamental freedoms and the dignity and worth of the human person;

WHEREAS the Parliament of Canada, being desirous of enshrining certain principles and the human rights and fundamental freedoms derived from them, enacted the Canadian Bill of Rights in order to ensure the protection of those rights and freedoms in Canada in matters coming within its legislative authority; and

WHEREAS the Legislature of Alberta, affirming those principles and recognizing the need to ensure the protection of those rights and freedoms in Alberta in matters coming within its legislative authority, desires to enact an Alberta Bill of Rights;

THEREFORE HER MAJESTY, by and with the advice and consent of the Legislative Assembly of Alberta, enacts as follows:

1. Recognition and declaration of rights and freedoms — It is hereby recognized and declared that in Alberta there exist without discrimination by reason of race, national origin, colour, religion or sex, the following human rights and fundamental freedoms, namely:

(*a*) the right of the individual to liberty, security of the person and enjoyment of property, and the right not to be deprived thereof except by due process of law;

(*b*) the right of the individual to equality before the law and the protection of the law;

(*c*) freedom of religion;

(*d*) freedom of speech;

(*e*) freedom of assembly and association;

(*f*) freedom of the press.

[1980, c. A-16, s. 1]

2.   The Saskatchewan Human Rights Code

S.S. 1979, c. S-24.1.

Part I

Bill of Rights

4. Right to freedom of conscience — Every person and every class of persons shall enjoy the right to freedom of conscience, opinion and belief and freedom of religious association, teaching, practice and worship.

5. Right to free expression — Every person and every class of persons shall, under the law, enjoy the right to freedom of expression through all means of communication, including, without limiting the generality of the foregoing, the arts, speech, the press or radio, television or any other broadcasting device.

6. Right to free association — Every person and every class of persons shall enjoy the right to peaceable assembly with others and to form with others associations of any character under the law.

7. Right to freedom from arbitrary imprisonment — Every person and every class of persons shall enjoy the right to freedom from arbitrary arrest or detention.

[1989-90, c. 23, s. 4]

8. Right to elections — Every qualified voter resident in Saskatchewan shall enjoy the right to exercise freely his or her franchise in all elections and shall possess the right to require that no Legislative Assembly shall continue for a period in excess of five years.

[2001, c. 26, s. 4]

3.   Quebec Charter of Human Rights and Freedoms

R.S.Q., c. C-12.

Part I

Human Rights and Freedoms

Chapter I

Fundamental Freedoms and Rights

1. Right to life — Every human being has a right to life, and to personal security, inviolability and freedom.

Juridical personality — He also possesses juridical personality.

[1975, c. 6, s. 1; 1982, c. 61, s. 1]

2. Right to assistance — Every human being whose life is in peril has a right to assistance.

Aiding person whose life is in peril — Every person must come to the aid of anyone whose life is in peril, either personally or calling for aid, by giving him the necessary and immediate physical assistance, unless it involves danger to himself or a third person, or he has another valid reason.

3. Fundamental freedoms — Every person is the possessor of the fundamental freedoms, including freedom of conscience, freedom of religion, freedom of opinion, freedom of expression, freedom of peaceful assembly and freedom of association.

[1975, c. 6, s. 3]

4. Safeguard of dignity — Every person has a right to the safeguard of his dignity, honour and reputation.

[1975, c. 6, s. 4]

5. Respect for private life — Every person has a right to respect for his private life.

[1975, c. 6, s. 5]

6. Peaceful enjoyment of property — Every person has a right to the peaceful enjoyment and free disposition of his property, except to the extent provided by law.

[1975, c. 6, s. 6]

7. Home inviolable — A person's home is inviolable.

[1975, c. 6, s. 7]

8. Respect for private property — No one may enter upon the property of another or take anything there from without his express or implied consent.

[1975, c. 6, s. 8]

9. Right to secrecy — Every person has a right to non-disclosure of confidential information.

Disclosure of confidential information — No person bound to professional secrecy by law and no priest or other minister of religion may, even in judicial proceedings, disclose confidential information revealed to him by reason of his position or profession, unless he is authorized to do so by the person who confided such information to him or by an express provision of law.

Duty of tribunal — The tribunal must, ex officio, ensure that professional secrecy is respected.

[1975, c. 6, s. 9]

4.   Yukon Human Rights Act

R.S.Y. 2002, c. 116.

Part 1

Bill of Rights

3. Right to freedom of religion and of conscience — Every individual and every group shall, in accordance with the law, enjoy the right to freedom of religion, conscience, opinion, and belief.

[R.S. Supp., c. 11, s. 3]

4. Right to freedom of expression — Every individual and every group shall, in accordance with the law, enjoy the right to freedom of expression, including freedom of the press and other media of communication.

[R.S. Supp., c. 11, s. 4]

5. Right to freedom of assembly and of association — Every individual and every group shall, in accordance with the law, enjoy the right to peaceable assembly with others and the right to form with others associations of any character.

[R.S. Supp., c. 11, s. 5]

6. Right to enjoyment and disposition of property — Every individual has a right to the peaceful enjoyment and free disposition of his or her property, except to the extent provided by law, and no one shall be deprived of that right except with just compensation.

[R.S. Supp., c. 11, s. 5.1]

(ii)   Preambles and Statements of Purpose

1.   Human Rights Code (British Columbia)

R.S.B.C. 1996, c. 210.

3. Purposes — The purposes of this Code are as follows:

(*a*) to foster a society in British Columbia in which there are no impediments to full and free participation in the economic, social, political and cultural life of British Columbia;

(*b*) to promote a climate of understanding and mutual respect where all are equal in dignity and rights;

(*c*) to prevent discrimination prohibited by this Code;

(*d*) to identify and eliminate persistent patterns of inequality associated with discrimination prohibited by this Code;

(*e*) to provide a means of redress for those persons who are discriminated against contrary to this Code;

(*f*) [Repealed: 2002-62-2.]

(*g*) [Repealed: 2002-62-2.]

[R.S.B.C. 1996 (Supp)-210-2 [S.B.C. 1995-42-3]; 2002-62-2]

2.   Human Rights, Citizenship and Multiculturalism Act (Alberta)

R.S.A. 2000, c. H-14.

Preamble

WHEREAS recognition of the inherent dignity and the equal and inalienable rights of all persons is the foundation of freedom, justice and peace in the world;

WHEREAS it is recognized in Alberta as a fundamental principle and as a matter of public policy that all persons are equal in: dignity, rights and responsibilities without regard to race, religious beliefs, colour, gender, physical disability, mental disability, age, ancestry, place of origin, marital status, source of income or family status;

WHEREAS multiculturalism describes the diverse racial and cultural composition of Alberta society and its importance is recognized in Alberta as a fundamental principle and a matter of public policy;

WHEREAS it is recognized in Alberta as a fundamental principle and as a matter of public policy that all Albertans should share in an awareness and appreciation of the diverse racial and cultural composition of society and that the richness of life in Alberta is enhanced by sharing that diversity; and

WHEREAS it is fitting that these principles be affirmed by the Legislature of Alberta in an enactment whereby those equality rights and that diversity may be protected:

3.   The Saskatchewan Human Rights Code

S.S. 1979, c. S-24.1

3. Objects — The objects of this Act are:

    (*a*) to promote recognition of the inherent dignity and the equal inalienable rights of all members of the human family; and

    (*b*) to further public policy in Saskatchewan that every person is free and equal in dignity and rights and to discourage and eliminate discrimination.

4.   The Human Rights Code (Manitoba)

C.C.S.M. c. H175.

WHEREAS Manitobans recognize the individual worth and dignity of every member of the human family, and this principle underlies the *Universal Declaration of Human Rights*, the *Canadian Charter of Rights and Freedoms*, and other solemn undertakings, international and domestic, that Canadians honour;

AND WHEREAS Manitobans recognize that

(*a*) implicit in the above principle is the right of all individuals to be treated in all matters solely on the basis of their personal merits, and to be accorded equality of opportunity with all other individuals;

(*b*) to protect this right it is necessary to restrict unreasonable discrimination against individuals, including discrimination based on stereotypes or generalizations about groups with whom they are or are thought to be associated, and to ensure that reasonable accommodation is made for those with special needs;

(*c*) in view of the fact that past discrimination against certain groups has resulted in serious disadvantage to members of those groups, and therefore it is important to provide for affirmative action programs and other special programs designed to overcome this historic disadvantage;

(*d*) much discrimination is rooted in ignorance and education is essential to its eradication, and therefore it is important that human rights educational programs assist Manitobans to understand all their fundamental rights and freedoms, as well as their corresponding duties and responsibilities to others; and

(*e*) these various protections for the human rights of Manitobans are of such fundamental importance that they merit paramount status over all other laws of the province; ...

5.   Human Rights Code (Ontario)

R.S.O. 1990, c. H.19.

Preamble

WHEREAS recognition of the inherent dignity and the equal and inalienable rights of all members of the human family is the foundation of freedom, justice and peace in the world and is in accord with the Universal Declaration of Human Rights as proclaimed by the United Nations;

AND WHEREAS it is public policy in Ontario to recognize the dignity and worth of every person and to provide for equal rights and opportunities without discrimination that is contrary to law, and having as its aim the creation of a climate of understanding and mutual respect for the dignity and worth of each person so that each person feels a part of the community and able to contribute fully to the development and well-being of the community and the Province;

AND WHEREAS these principles have been confirmed in Ontario by a number of enactments of the Legislature and it is desirable to revise and extend the protection of human rights in Ontario; ...

6.   Quebec Charter of Human Rights and Freedoms

R.S.Q., c. C-12.

Preamble

WHEREAS every human being possesses intrinsic rights and freedoms designed to ensure his protection and development;

Whereas all human beings are equal in worth and dignity, and are entitled to equal protection of the law;

Whereas respect for the dignity of the human being and recognition of his rights and freedoms constitute the foundation of justice and peace;

Whereas the rights and freedoms of the human person are inseparable from the rights and freedoms of others and from the common well-being;

Whereas it is expedient to solemnly declare the fundamental human rights and freedoms in a Charter, so that they may be guaranteed by the collective will and better protected against any violation; ...

7.   Human Rights Act (New Brunswick)

R.S.N.B. 1973, c. H-11.

WHEREAS recognition of the fundamental principle that all persons are equal in dignity and human rights without regard to race, colour, religion, national origin, ancestry, place of origin, age, physical disability, mental disability, marital status, sexual orientation, sex, social condition, political belief or activity, is a governing principle sanctioned by the laws of New Brunswick; and

WHEREAS ignorance, forgetfulness, or contempt of the rights of others are often the causes of public miseries and social disadvantage; and

WHEREAS people and institutions remain free only when freedom is founded upon respect for moral and spiritual values and the rule of law; and

WHEREAS it is recognized that human rights must be guaranteed by the rule of law, and that these principles have been confirmed in New Brunswick by a number of enactments of this Legislature; and

WHEREAS it is desirable to enact a measure to codify and extend such enactments and to simplify their administration;

THEREFORE her Majesty, by and with the advice and consent of the Legislative Assembly of New Brunswick, enacts as follows:

[1985, c. 30, s. 2; 1992, c. 30, s. 1; 2004, c. 21, s. 1]

8.   Human Rights Act (Nova Scotia)

R.S.N.S. 1989, c. 214.

2. Purpose of Act — The purpose of this Act is to

(a) recognize the inherent dignity and the equal and inalienable rights of all members of the human family;

(b) proclaim a common standard for achievement of basic human rights by all Nova Scotians;

(c) recognize that human rights must be protected by the rule of law;

(d) affirm the principle that every person is free and equal in dignity and rights;

(e) recognize that the government, all public agencies and all persons in the Province have the responsibility to ensure that every individual in the Province is afforded an equal opportunity to enjoy a full and productive life and that failure to provide equality of opportunity threatens the status of all persons; and

(f) extend the statute law relating to human rights and to provide for its effective administration.

[1991, c. 12, s. 1]

9.   Human Rights Act (Prince Edward Island)

R.S.P.E.I. 1988, c. H-12.

WHEREAS recognition of the inherent dignity and the equal and inalienable rights of all members of the human family is the foundation of freedom, justice and peace in the world and is in accord with the Universal Declaration of Human Rights as proclaimed by the United Nations;

AND WHEREAS it is recognized in Prince Edward Island as a fundamental principle that all persons are equal in dignity and human rights without regard to race, religion, creed, color, sex, marital status, or ethnic or national origin;

AND WHEREAS in 1968 *An Act Respecting Human Rights* was passed by the legislature of this province in response to the Universal Declaration of Human Rights passed by the General Assembly of the United Nations;

AND WHEREAS the principles contained in *An Act Respecting Human Rights* require amplification;

AND WHEREAS it is deemed desirable to provide for the people of the province a Human Rights Commission to which complaints relating to discrimination may be made: ...

10.   Human Rights Act (Northwest Territories)

S.N.W.T. 2002, c. 18.

Whereas recognition of the inherent dignity and the equal and inalienable rights of all members of the human family is the foundation of freedom, justice and peace in the world and is in accord with the Universal Declaration of Human Rights as proclaimed by the United Nations;

And whereas it is recognized in the Northwest Territories that every individual is free and equal in dignity and rights without regard to his or her race, colour, ancestry, nationality, ethnic origin, place of origin, creed, religion, age, disability, sex, sexual orientation, gender identity, marital status, family status, family affiliation, political belief, political association or social condition and without regard to whether he or she has had a conviction for which a pardon has been granted;

And whereas it is of vital importance to promote respect for and observance of human rights in the Northwest Territories, including the rights and freedoms protected under the Canadian Charter of Rights and Freedoms, and rights and freedoms protected under international human rights instruments, while at the same time promoting respect for, and the observance of, the rights and freedoms of aboriginal peoples that are recognized and affirmed under the Constitution of Canada;

And whereas it is recognized that every person, having duties to others and to the community to which he or she belongs, is responsible to strive for the promotion and observance of the rights recognized in this Act; ...

11. Human Rights Act (Nunavut)

S.Nu. 2003, c. 12.

Whereas it is just and consistent with Canada's international undertakings to recognize and make special provision for Inuit culture and values that underlie the Inuit way of life;

Whereas recognition of the inherent dignity and the equal and inalienable rights of all members of the human family is the foundation of freedom, justice and peace in the world and is in accord with the Universal Declaration of Human Rights as proclaimed by the United Nations;

And whereas human rights must be protected by the rule of law; ...

12. Human Rights Act (Yukon)

R.S.Y. 2002, c. 116.

Preamble

Recognizing that respect for human rights is a fundamental part of Canada's heritage,

That Canada is a party to the United Nations' *Universal Declaration of Human Rights* and other international undertakings having as their object the improvement of human rights in Canada and other nations of the world,

That the Yukon Government has a responsibility to encourage an understanding and recognition of human rights that is consistent with Canada's international undertakings and with the initiatives taken by Canada and the provinces, and

That it is just and consistent with Canada's international undertakings to recognize and make special provision for the unique needs and cultural heritage of the aboriginal peoples of the Yukon,

The Commissioner of the Yukon Territory, by and with the advice and consent of the Legislative Assembly, enacts as follows:

1. Objects — (1) The objects of this Act are

(a) to further in the Yukon the public policy that every individual is free and equal in dignity and rights;

(b) to discourage and eliminate discrimination;

(c) to promote recognition of the inherent dignity and worth and of the equal and inalienable rights of all members of the human family, these being principles underlying the *Canadian Charter of Rights and Freedoms* and the *Universal Declaration of Human Rights* and other solemn undertakings, international and national, which Canada honours.

(2) This Act does not affect rights pertaining to aboriginal peoples established by the Constitution of Canada or by a land claims agreement.

[R.S., Supp., c. 11, s. 1]

2. Multi-cultural heritage — This Act shall be interpreted in a manner consistent with the preservation and enhancement of the multi-cultural heritage of the residents of the Yukon.

[R.S., Supp., c. 11, s. 2]

Some Useful References

Alfredsson, Gudmundur & Asbjørn Eide, eds., *The Universal Declaration of Human Rights: A Common Standard of Achievement* (The Hague: Martinus Nijhoff, 1999).

Bayefsky, Anne F., *International Human Rights Law: Use in Canadian Charter of Rights and Freedoms Litigation* (Toronto: Butterworths, 1992).

Conde, H. Victor, *A Handbook of International Human Rights Terminology* (Lincoln: University of Nebraska Press, 1999).

Donnelly, Jack, *Universal Human Rights In Theory & Practice*, Second Edition (Ithaca: Cornell University Press, 2002).

Freeman, Mark & Gibran van Ert, *International Human Rights Law* (Toronto: Irwin Law, 2004).

Freeman, Mark and Gibran van Ert, *International Human Rights Law: Texts, Cases, and Materials* (Toronto: Irwin Law, 2005).

Gane, Christopher & Mark Mackare, eds., *Human Rights and the Administration of Justice: International Instruments* (The Hague: Kluwer, 1997).

Ishay, Micheline R., *The History of Human Rights: From Ancient Times to the Globalization Era* (Berkeley: University of California Press, 2004).

Jayawickrama, Nihal, *The Judicial Application of Human Rights Law* (Cambridge: Cambridge University Press, 2003).

Lawson, Edward, *Encyclopedia of Human Rights*, 2d ed. (Washington, D.C.: Taylor & Francis, 1996).

McCorquodale, Robert, ed., *Human Rights* (Aldershot: Ashgate Publishing, 2003).

Morsink, Johannes, *The Universal Declaration of Human Rights: Origins, Drafting & Intent* (Philadelphia: University of Pennsylvania, 1999).

Schabas, William A., *International Human Rights and the Canadian Charter*, 2d ed. (Toronto: Thomson Carswell, 1996).

Steiner, Henry J. & Philip Alston, *International Human Rights in Context: Law, Politics, Morals*, 2d ed., (Oxford: Oxford University Press, 2000).

van Ert, Gibran, *Using International Law in Canadian Courts* (The Hague: Kluwer, 2002).

INDEX